COLLINS

GW01393062

BEL

STREETFINDER
ATLAS

Legend

Principal Classified Routes		//////////	Pedestrianised Area
A2 *B170* Official Road Numbers			City Boundary
→ One Way Streets		BT 7	Postal Districts
Railways & Stations			

Scale 4¼ inches to 1 mile

0   ¼   ½ mile
0   500   1000 metres

Published by Collins
An imprint of HarperCollins*Publishers*
77-85 Fulham Palace Road, Hammersmith, London W6 8JB

The HarperCollins website address is: www.**fire**and**water**.com

Copyright © HarperCollins*Publishers* Ltd 1997
Mapping © Bartholomew Ltd 1990, 1994, 1995, 1997

Collins® is a registered trade mark of HarperCollins*Publishers* Limited

Mapping generated from Bartholomew digital databases

Based upon the Ordnance Survey Mapping with the permission of the Controller of Her Majesty's Staionery Office © Crown Copyright. Permit number 1318

Printed in Italy   ISBN 0 00 448675 7   UNL   e-mail: roadcheck@harpercollins.co.uk

HarperCollins*Publishers*

KEY TO MAP PAGES

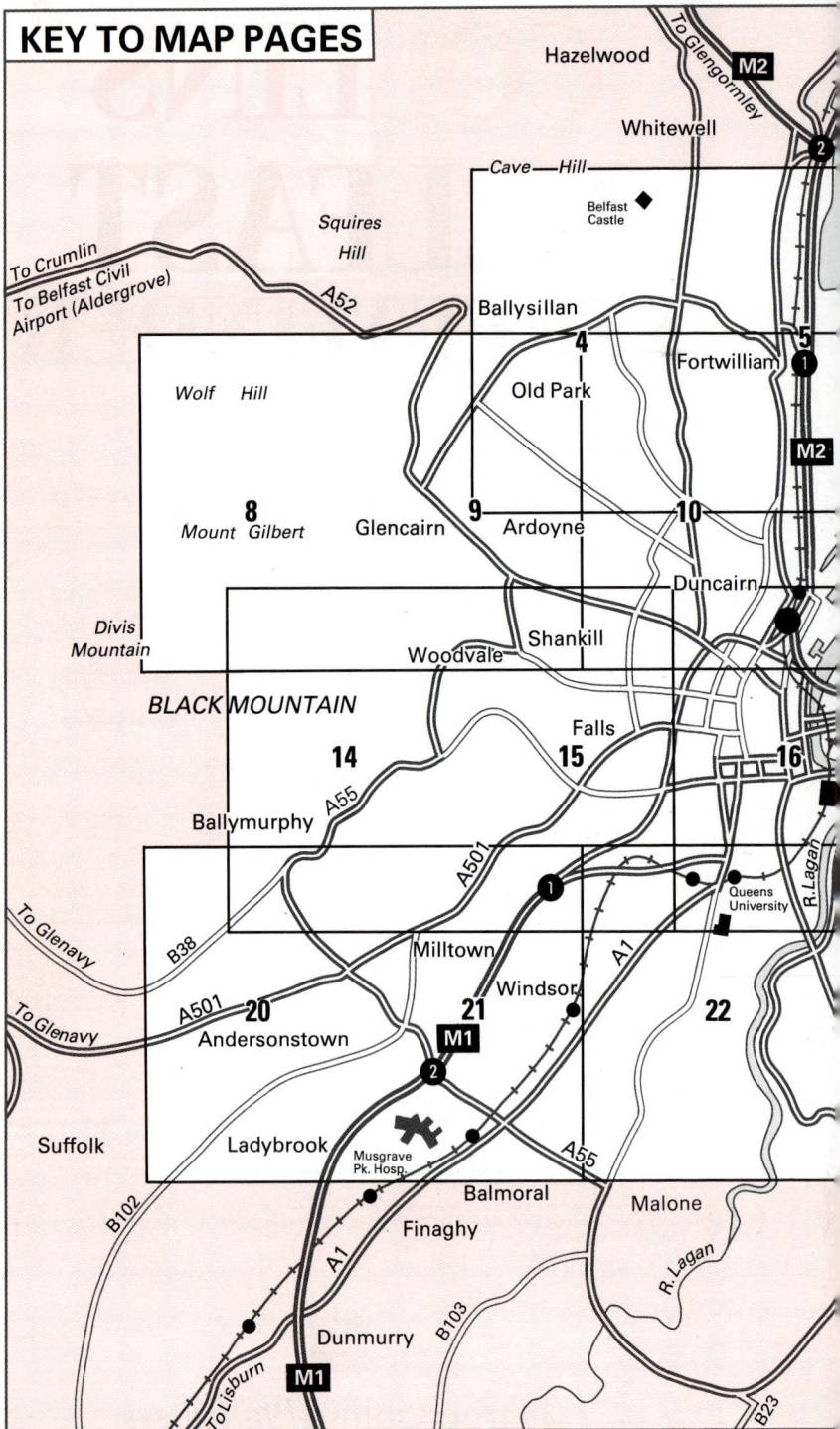

Hazelwood

To Glengormley

M2

Whitewell

2

Cave — Hill

Belfast Castle ◆

Squires Hill

To Crumlin

To Belfast Civil Airport (Aldergrove)

A52

Ballysillan

4

Fortwilliam

5

1

Wolf Hill

Old Park

M2

8

Mount Gilbert

Glencairn

9

Ardoyne

10

Duncairn

Divis Mountain

Shankill

Woodvale

BLACK MOUNTAIN

Falls

14

A55

15

16

Ballymurphy

A501

M1

To Glenavy

B38

1

Queens University

R.Lagan

Milltown

A1

To Glenavy

A501

20

Windsor

21

M1

22

Andersonstown

2

Suffolk

Ladybrook

Musgrave Pk. Hosp.

A55

Balmoral

Malone

B102

Finaghy

A1

R.Lagan

B103

Dunmurry

M1

To Lisburn

B23

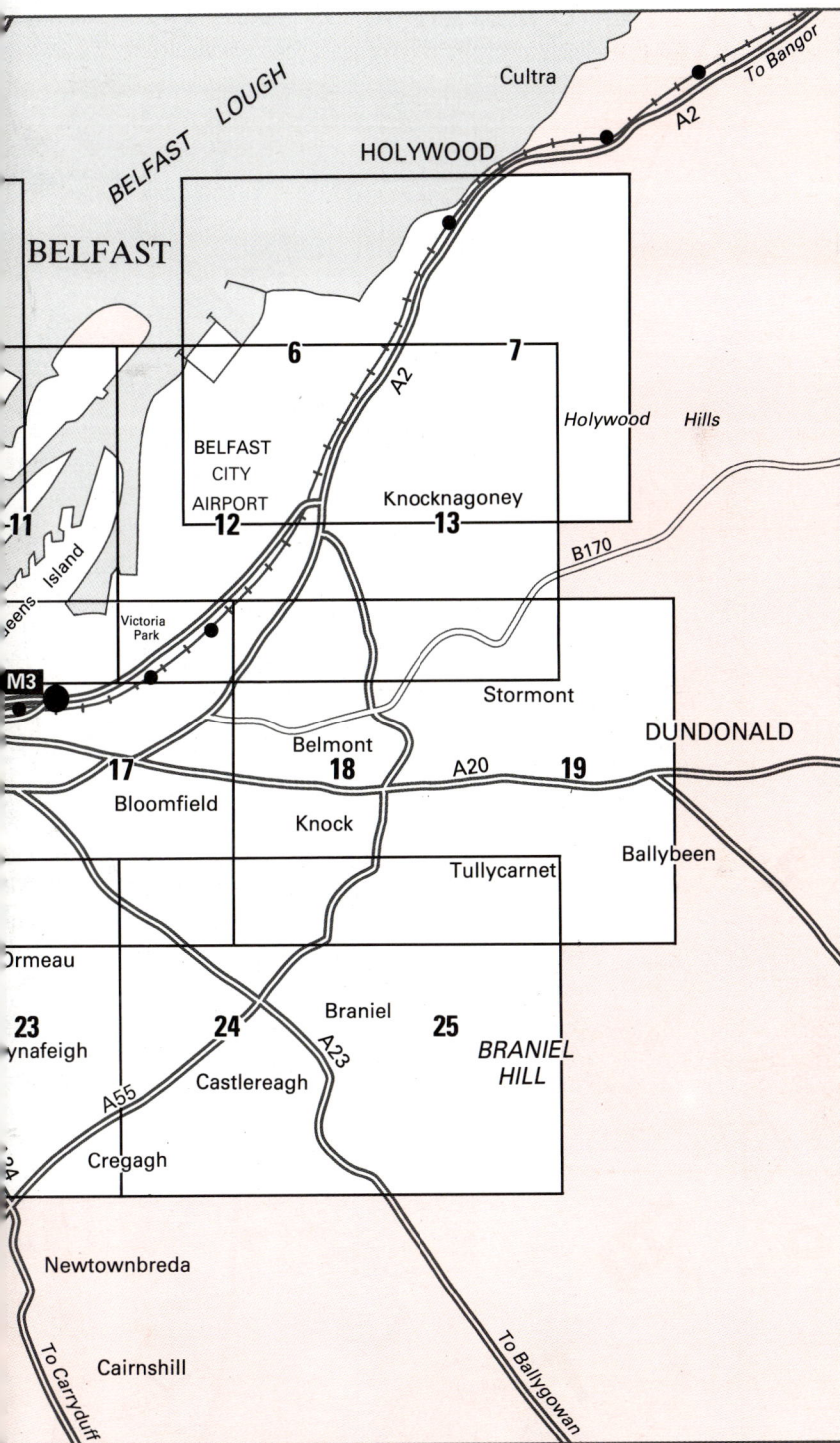

BELFAST LOUGH

Cultra

HOLYWOOD

BELFAST

To Bangor

A2

6

A2

7

Holywood   Hills

BELFAST
CITY
AIRPORT

-11

Knocknagoney

-12

13

B170

Queens   Island

Victoria
Park

Stormont

M3

DUNDONALD

Belmont

17

A20

19

Bloomfield

18

Knock

Ballybeen

Tullycarnet

Ormeau

Braniel

23

24

25

BRANIEL
HILL

ynafeigh

A23

A55

Castlereagh

24

Cregagh

Newtownbreda

To Carryduff

Cairnshill

To Ballygowan

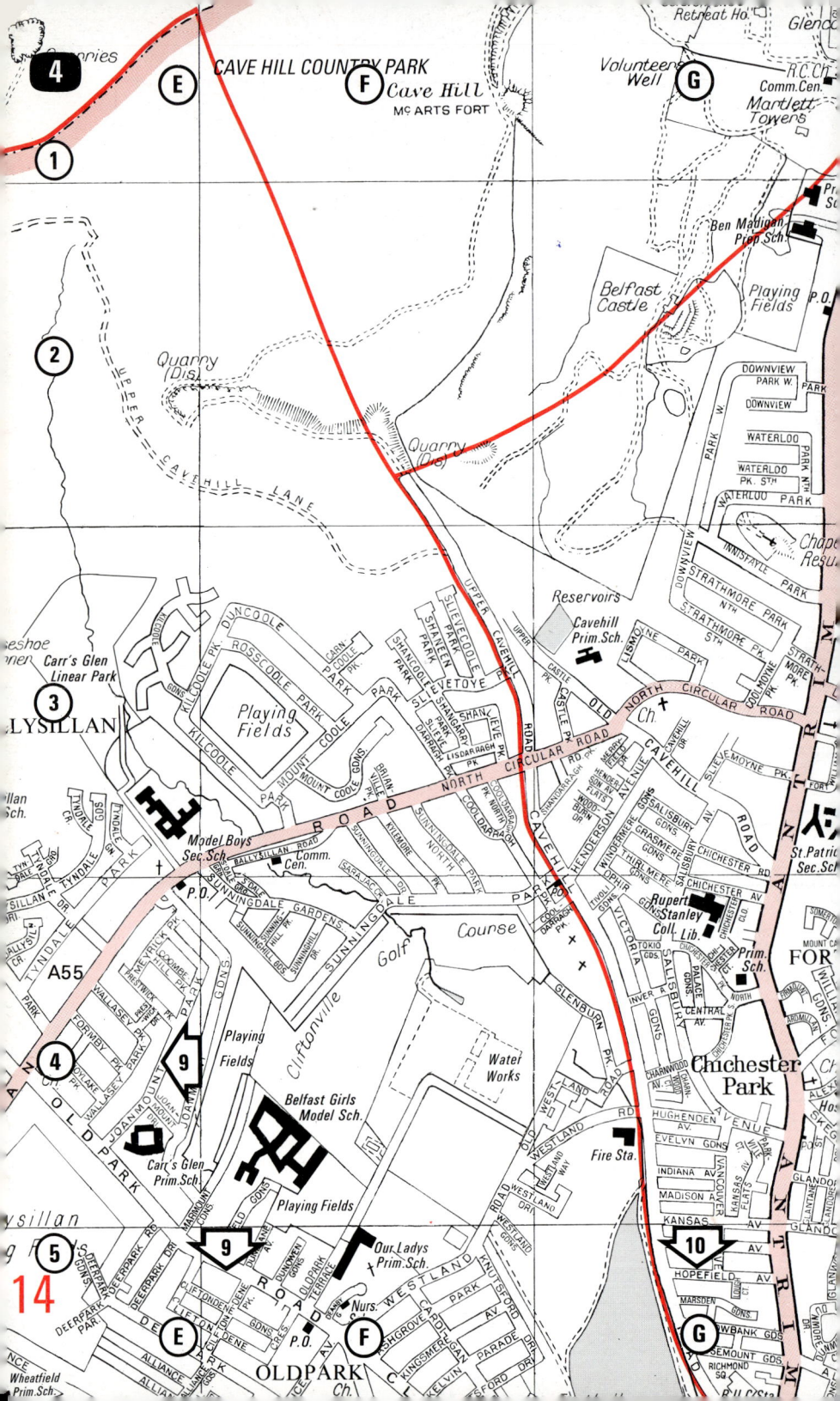

E F CAVE HILL COUNTRY PARK Cave Hill G

Retreat Ho. Glencb

Volunteers Well

R.C.Ch
Comm. Cen.
Martlett Towers

Mc ARTS FORT

1

Ben Madigan Prep. Sch.

Pri Sc

Belfast Castle

Playing Fields

P.O.

2

Quarry (Dis)

DOWNVIEW PARK W.
DOWNVIEW

WATERLOO PARK
WATERLOO PK. STH.
WATERLOO PARK

Quarry (Dis)

Reservoirs

Cavehill Prim. Sch.

Chape Resu

UPPER CAVEHILL LANE

INNISFAYLE PARK

STRATHMORE PARK NTH.
STRATHMORE PK. STH.
STRATHMORE PK.

LISMOYNE PARK

Carr's Glen Linear Park

seshoe

3

LYSILLAN

DUNCOOLE PK.
ROSSCOOLE PARK
KILCOOLE PK.
Playing Fields
MOUNT COOLE PARK
KILCOOLE PARK

CARN COOLE PK.
SHANCOOLE PK.
SLIEVECOOLE PK.
LEVETOYE
STANEEN

UPPER CAVEHILL

CASTLE PK.
OLD CASTLE RD.
NORTH CIRCULAR ROAD

Ch.

CAVEHILL DR.
SLIEVEMOYNE PK.

St. Patric Sec. Sch.

FOR

llan Sch.

NORTH CIRCULAR ROAD

Model Boys Sec. Sch.
Comm. Cen.
BALLYSILLAN ROAD
P.O.

MOUNT COOLE GDNS.
SUNNINGDALE NORTH
KILMORE PK.
SARAJAC PK.
COOLDARRAGH

CAVEHILL ROAD

HENDERSON AVENUE
SALISBURY AV.
CHICHESTER
GRASMERE GDNS.
HIRLMERE
CHICHESTER

Rupert Stanley Coll. Lib.
Prim. Sch.

SUNNINGDALE GARDENS
SUNNINGHILL

SUNNINGDALE

Golf Course

CAVEHILL ROAD

TOKIO GDNS.
SALISBURY
PALACE GDNS.

A55

MEYRICK PK.
WALLASEY PK.
FORMBY PK.

JOANMOUNT

Playing Fields

4

9

Clftonville

Water Works

GLENBURN

INVER GDNS.
CENTRAL AV.

Chichester Park

OLD PARK

Belfast Girls Model Sch.

Carr's Glen Prim. Sch.

Playing Fields

HUGHENDEN AV.
EVELYN GDNS.
INDIANA AV.
MADISON AV.
KANSAS

WESTLAND ROAD
WESTLAND WAY
WESTLAND GDNS.

Fire Sta.

CHARNWOOD AV.

ysillan

g F

5

14

DEERPARK RD.
DEERPARK PARK

CLIFTONDENE GDNS.
CLIFTONDENE
DUNOWEN GDNS.
OLDPARK TERRACE

ROAD

Our Ladys Prim. Sch.
Nurs. Sch.
P.O.

E F

WESTLAND ROAD
KNUTSFORD PARK
KINGSMERE
ASHGROVE PARK

9

10
HOPEFIELD

MARSDEN GDNS.
WYNBANK GDNS.
SEMOUNT GDNS.
RICHMOND SQ.

G

OLDPARK Ch.

Wheatfield Prim. Sch.
ALLIANCE

Greencastle

H Cedar Lodge Special Sch.
Hazelwood Integrated Coll.

GRAYMOUNT
GRAYMOUNT PARK
GRAYMOUNT DR

GREEN
CASTLE
CLO.

GREEN
Sch.
R.C. Ch.
RUC Sta

J

K

1

2

Fortwilliam Golf Course

St. Mary's Pr. Sch

Youth Club

GREEN
CASTLE
PL.

DOWN
VIEW
GDNS
DOWN
VIEW MS.

SHORE CRESCENT

Ch.

2

NEW AVENUE

PARKMOUNT TER
PARKMOUNT
PT. PLAS

INNISFAYLE

ROAD
GDNS

CASTLE GDNS

DONEGAL
INNIS-
FAYLE
DRIVE

CASTLE
DR
FAIRHILL
GDNS
FAIRHILL
DR
WAVENEY
GR

PARK
FAIRHILL
WK.

P.O.

WAV
HTS

SHORE
CRESC

Loughside
Park

PK

CASTLE AV.

CASTLE

FAIRHILL

LANSDOWNE
PK

SHERINGHURST
PK

M 2

ASHLEY
GDNS

ROAD

BRISTOL AV

TAUNTON AV

LANSDOWNE

Lowwood
Pr. Schs.
LOWWOOD

VERNON DR

VERNON
PARK

Loughside
Recreation
Centre

Playing
Fields

3

SOMERTON

ALEXANDER

LANS
DOWNE

LANSDOWNE
PK
ROAD

MT. VERNON DR

MT. VERNON

MT VERNON PK

Ch

Little Flower
Girls
Sec. Sch.
R.C.
Dominican
College
LIAM

A55

PORT ORANGE ST

1

DARGAN

DUNCRUE
CRES.

DARGAN
ROAD

CRES

11

DARGAN

4

Ch.

DUNLAMBERT

DUNLAMBERT
DRIVE

Ch.

OAKMOUNT
DRI

Shopping
Centre

YORK PK
YORK CR
YORK PAR
YORK DR

DUNCRUE
PLACE

DUNCRUE
ROAD

CRES

SHORE
ROAD

Castle
High Sch.

Prim
Sch.

SEAVIEW
DRIVE

SEAVIEW

SOMERTON
GDNS

PREMIER DR

Norwood
Linear Pk.

WOOD PK

DUNCRUE LINK

MINERAL
ST

DUNCRUE

ST VINCENT ST

5

ARDAVON PK

SOMERTON
ROAD

JELLICOE
DRIVE

VICTORIA
PK

FORTWILL

WOOD PK

IN WOOD
PAR

P.O.

ST AUBYN ST

SEAL

HERBIAN

Res

Sewage
Works

K

FORTWILLIAM

ASHFIELD
GDNS

10

WOOD
GDNS

ST. VINCENT'S ST
ST DEMPSEY'S
HARRISBURG
PITTSBURG
ROSA ST

DUNCRUE

SKEGONEILL

11

DUNCRUE STREET

BT 15

H

Football

Clinic &
Lib
Youth &
Comm. Cen.

The Grove
Playing Fields

SKEGONEILL

J

M 2

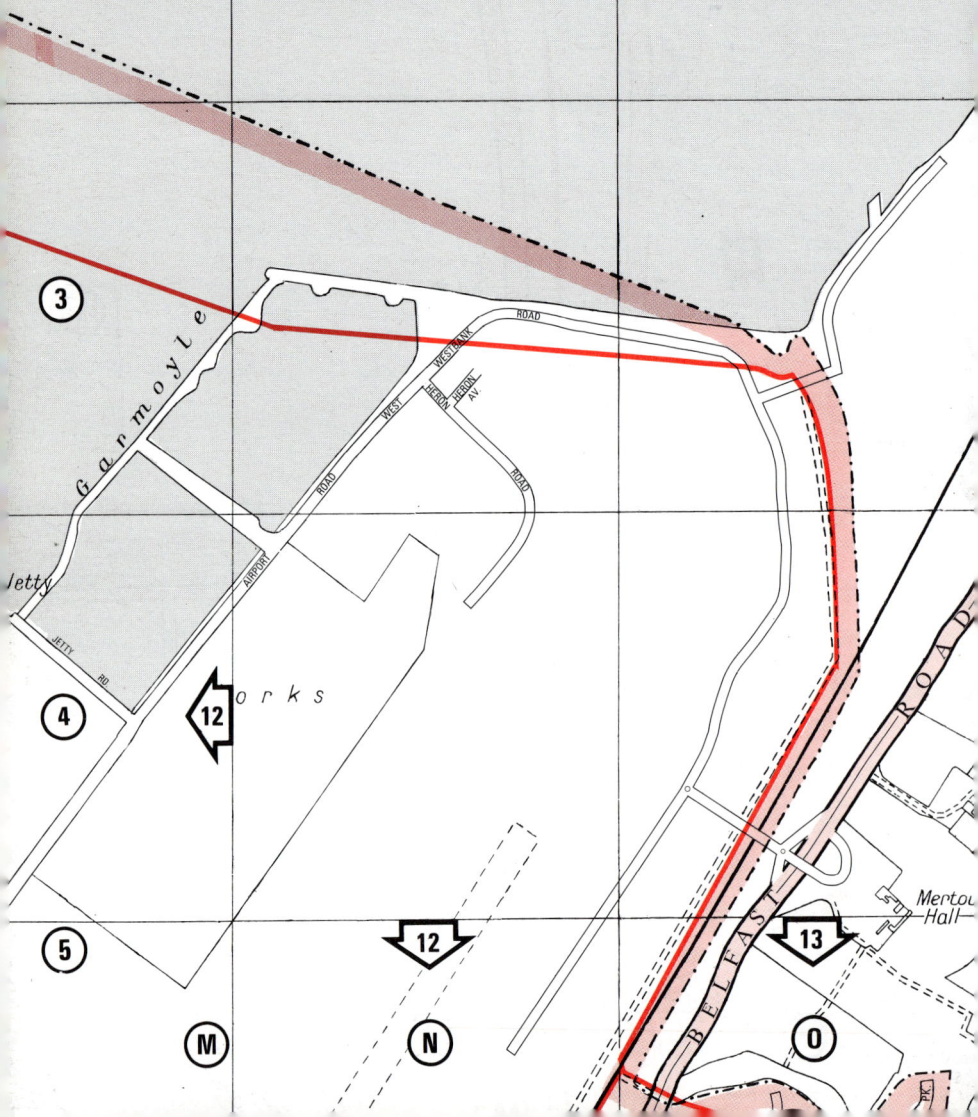

M

N

O

1

2

3

Garmoyle

Jetty

JETTY RD

4

12

orks

5

12

M

N

ROAD

WEST HERON HERON AV.

WESTBANK

ROAD

AIRPORT ROAD

BELFAST ROAD

Mertou Hall

13

O

HOLYWOOD

HOLYWOOD

BT 18

Marino House
Benedar
Seapark Rec. Grd
N.I.R.
BANGOR
Ballymenoch Park

P   Q   R

1
2
3
4
5

Landing Stage
Bangor Rd
Tudor Park
Ch.
Martello Ter
Priory Pk.
Tudor Dais
Croft
Glen

SHORE RD
STRAND
Marine Parade
Esplanade
The Cts
Victoria Rd
Church Rd
Brook St
Church St
Claremont Rd
Ardmore
Eliza-Beth Rd
Princes
Kinnegar
The Rd
Byron
R.U.C. Sta.
Fire Sta.
Lib.
Church View
Spencer St
Church Gdn.
Ch. Sch.
Marmion
Ardmore Av.
Glenview Av.

Spafield Playing Fields
HIGH STREET
Downshire Rd
R.C. Ch. & Pr. Sch.
Trevor St
Park
Hillview Pl.
Demesne Rd
Windsor
Glenlyon Park
Kerr Park
Craigtara
Holywood High Sch.
Lady's
Mile
Alexandra Park
Lemon Av.
Field Av.
Demesne
St. Valentine's
Sacred Heart of Mary Convent
Abbey
North Link
West Av.
Carnend
Priory Link
Ring
P.O.
The Gro
Woodend
Abbots
Sullivan Upper School
Mile
Winshill
Demesne
Pine Crest
Golf Course
Quarry (Disused)
Filter Beds
BELFAST RD
Strandburn Rd
Jacksons Rd
West Green
Beech Av.
Oakley
The Green
Ring
South Ring
Arragreena Rd
Demesne Rd
Walk
Nun's
Holywood
Holywood Hill House
Reservoir
Mote Lands
Redburn Prim. Sch.
Playing Field
Andtullagh
Club Ho.
Firmount
Palace Gdns
Crescent
Cemetery
Redburn
Maryfield
Rorys Wood
Redburn Country Park
13
Holywood   Moss
P   Q   R

8

A B C

3

Quarry (Dis)

Mill Pond

Wolfhill Flax Spinning Mill

Wolfhill House

WOLFHILL GRD

WOLFHILL DR

WOLFHILL

MILL AV.

MILL AV.

Mill Pond

Mill Pond

Legoniel Br.

LEVER ST

LEGONAVEA

LIGONIE

LEGONIEL R

LEGONIEL R

LEGONIEL GDNS

4 Wolf Hill

RAVE

Wolfhill Villa

Glenside

LEGONIEL Ce

Crow Glen

Mill Race

Forth

River

FORTHRIVER P

5

ROAD

Mount Gilbert

STANDING STONE

GLENCAIR

Monks Hill

River

6 DIVIS
UNTAIN

Ballygomartin

Ba

The Forkings

7

14

A B C

Loughvie

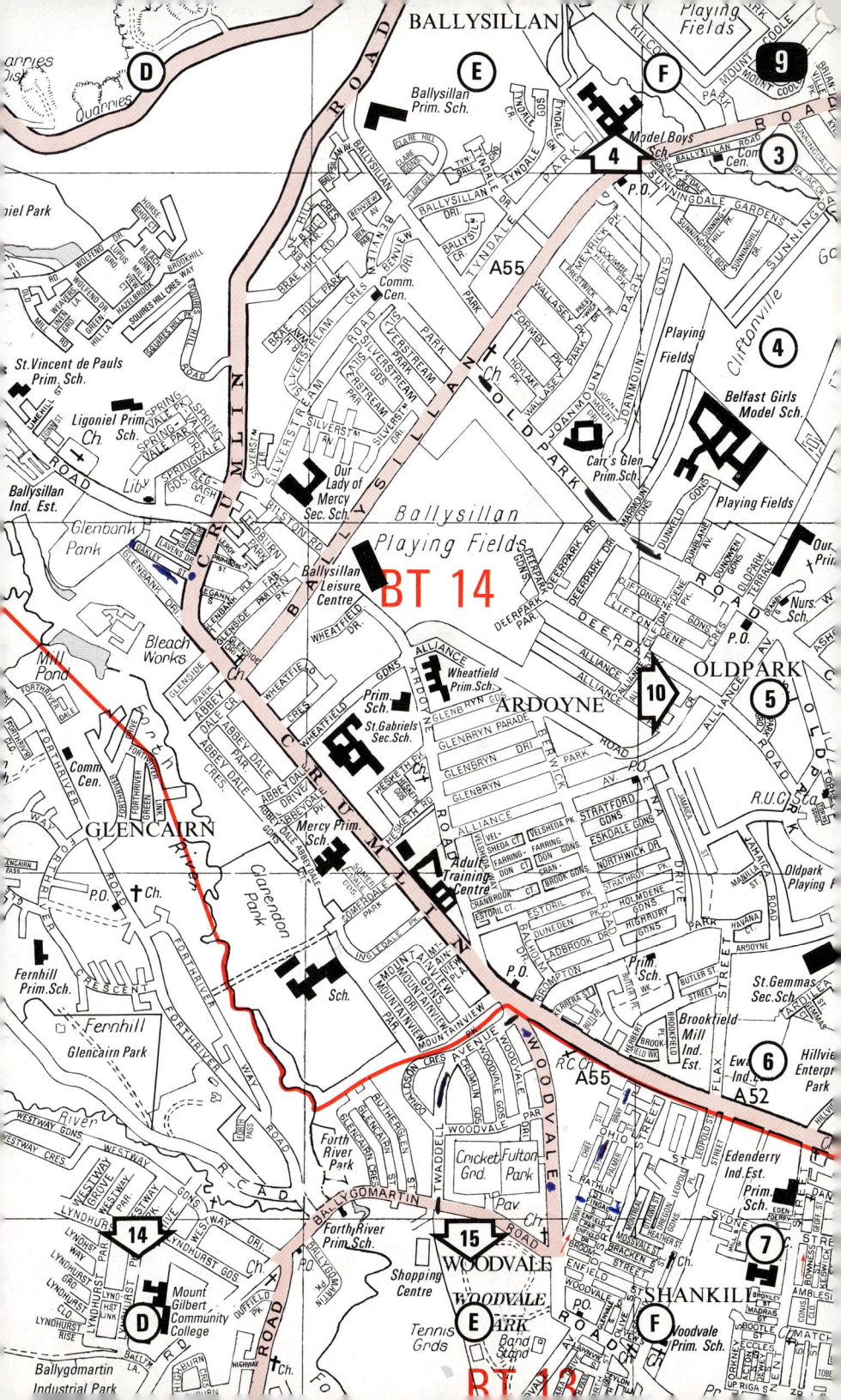

BALLYSILLAN

9

D   E   F

Ballysillan Prim. Sch.

Model Boys Sch.
Comm. Cen.
4   3

A55

CLARE HILL
TYNDALE
BALLYSILLAN DRI.
BALLYSILLAN CR.
BENVIEW
SUNNINGDALE GARDENS
SUNNINGDALE DR.

Comm. Cen.

MEYRICK
WALLASEY
HORMBY

Cliftonville

4

St. Vincent de Pauls Prim. Sch.

Ligoniel Prim. Sch.
Ch.
SPRING VALE
SPRINGVALE PAR.

SILVERSTREAM

Our Lady of Mercy Sec. Sch.

Playing Fields

Belfast Girls Model Sch.

Playing Fields

Ballysillan Ind. Est.

Glenbank Park

Lib.y

CRUMLIN ROAD

BALLYSILLAN ROAD

OLDPARK ROAD

Carr's Glen Prim. Sch.

Our Prim.

Ballysillan Leisure Centre

Ballysillan Playing Fields

DEERPARK

CLIFTONDENE
CLIFTONPARK
OLDPARK TERRACE

Nurs. Sch.
P.O.

OLDPARK

Bleach Works

Mill Pond

WHEATFIELD

Wheatfield Prim. Sch.

Prim. Sch.

St. Gabriels Sec. Sch.

GLENBRYN
ARDOYNE

GLENBRYN PARADE
BERWICK PARK
GLENBRYN DRI.
GLENBRYN AV.

10   5

ALLIANCE

ALLIANCE GDNS
ARDOYNE

ABBEY DALE
ABBEYDALE PAR.
ABBEYDALE CRES.
ABBEYDALE DRIVE

R.U.C. Sta.

Oldpark Playing F.

Comm. Cen.

GLENCAIRN

FORTHRIVER

Clarendon Park

Mercy Prim. Sch.

ALLIANCE

VELSHEDA PK.
VELSHEDA CT.
FARRING DON
STRATFORD GDNS
ESKDALE GDNS
NORTHWICK DR.
STRATHROY PK.
HIGHBURY GDNS
HOLMDENE GDNS

Adult Training Centre

CRANBROOK CT.
ESTORIL CT.
DUNEDEN PK.
LADBROOK DRO
BROMPTON

P.O.

Prim. Sch.

St. Gemmas Sec. Sch.

FLAX STREET

P.O.

Fernhill Prim. Sch.

Sch.

MOUNTAINVIEW GDNS
MOUNTAINVIEW DRI.
MOUNTAINVIEW PAR.

R.C.

A55

Brookfield Mill Ind. Est.

6

Hillview Enterpr. Park

Fernhill
Glencairn Park

FORTHRIVER WAY

WOODVALE AVENUE
WOODVALE ROAD

A52

Edenderry Ind. Est.
Prim. Sch.

Eden. Ind. Est.

WESTWAY GDNS
WESTWAY CRES
WESTWAY GROVE
WESTWAY PAR.

LYNDHURST

Forth River Park

Cricket Grd.
Fulton Park
Pav.

WOODVALE

OHIO ST.
RATHLIN ST.

RC

Ch.

SHANKILL

7

14

LYNDHURST GDNS
LYNDHURST DRI.

Mount Gilbert Community College

Forth River Prim. Sch.

BALLYGOMARTIN ROAD
TWADDELL

15   WOODVALE

Shopping Centre

WOODVALE PARK

WOODVALE Prim. Sch.

D   E   F

Tennis Grds
Band Stand

Ballygomartin Industrial Park

BT 14

BT 13

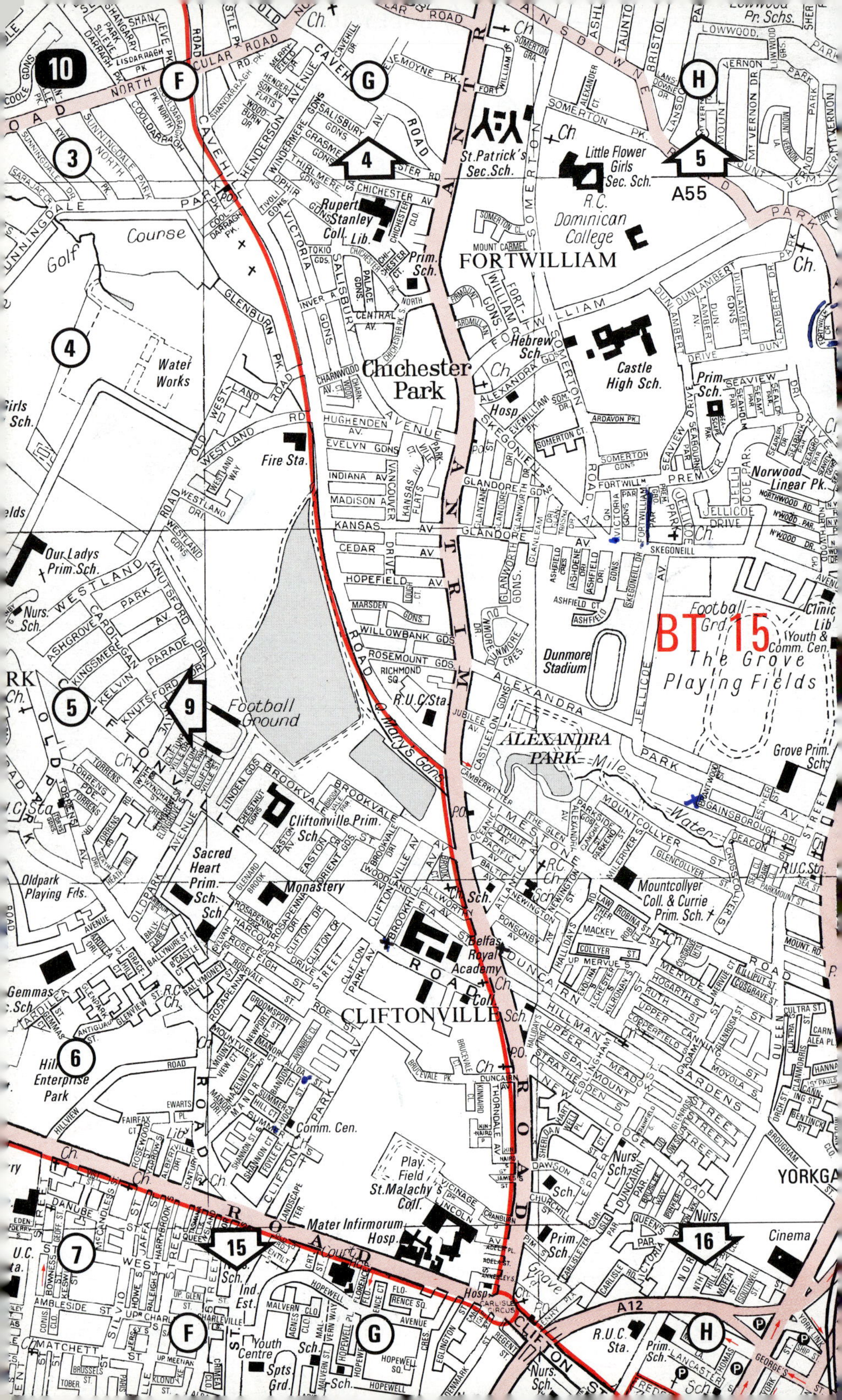

Grid references (top row, left to right)
10, F, G, **4**, H, **5**, A55

Districts / Major labels
FORTWILLIAM
Chichester Park
ALEXANDRA PARK
CLIFTONVILLE
BT 15
The Grove Playing Fields
YORKGATE

Schools, colleges and institutions
- St Patrick's Sec. Sch.
- Little Flower Girls Sec. Sch.
- R.C. Dominican College
- Rupert Stanley Coll. Lib.
- Prim. Sch.
- Hebrew Sch.
- Mount Carmel
- Castle High Sch.
- Prim. Sch.
- Norwood Linear Pk.
- Our Ladys Prim. Sch.
- Nurs. Sch.
- Football Grd.
- Youth & Comm. Cen.
- Clinic Lib.
- Grove Prim. Sch.
- Dunmore Stadium
- Cliftonville Prim. Sch.
- Sacred Heart Prim. Sch.
- Monastery
- Oldpark Playing Flds.
- Belfast Royal Academy
- Mountcollyer Coll. & Currie Prim. Sch.
- Gemmas Sch.
- Hill Enterprise Park
- Comm. Cen.
- Play. Field
- St Malachy's Coll.
- Mater Infirmorum Hosp.
- Cinema
- Youth Centre
- Spts. Grd.
- Nurs. Sch.
- R.U.C. Sta.
- Prim. Sch.
- Girls Sch.

Other features
- Golf Course
- Water Works
- Fire Sta.
- Football Ground
- R.U.C. Sta.
- Hosp.
- Sacred Heart

Selected street / avenue names
Caven Road, Henderson Avenue, Salisbury Gdns, Grasmere Av, Windemere Gdns, Thirlmere Gdns, Chichester Gdns, Victoria Gdns, Salisbury Av, Palace Gdns, Inver Av, Central Av, North, Charnwood Av, Hughenden Av, Evelyn Gdns, Indiana Av, Madison Av, Vancouver Dr, Kansas Av, Cedar Av, Hopefield Av, Marsden Gdns, Willowbank Gdns, Rosemount Gdns, Richmond Sq, Westland Road, Westland Drive, Westland Way, Knutsford Dr, Ashgrove Park, Cardigan Park, Kingsmere Av, Kelvin Parade, Cliftonville, Brookvale Av, Eastland, Cliftonville Rd, Oldpark Road, Torrens Rd, Glandore Av, Skegoneill Av, Somerton Rd, Fortwilliam Park, Antrim Road, Alexandra Park, Jellicoe Av, Seaview, Gainsborough Dr, Mountcollyer Rd, Glencollyer St, Collyer St, Newington, Hallidays Rd, Hillman St, Upper Meadow St, Hogarths Rd, Duncairn Gdns, Strathroy, Mervue St, Lilliput St, Cosgrave St, Queen St, Limestone Road, Danube St, Glenbank, Baltic Av, Rosehead St, Harcourt, Kinnaird, Duncairn Av, Thorndale Av, Cranburn St, Carlisle, Clifton St, Lincoln Av, Agnes St, Hopewell Av, Malvern, Upper Charleville St, Ambleside St, Ewarts Pl, Fairfax, Cliftonpark Av, Glenrosa St, North Queen Street, Clifton Road, A12

(Map area — Belfast street atlas, grid page 10)

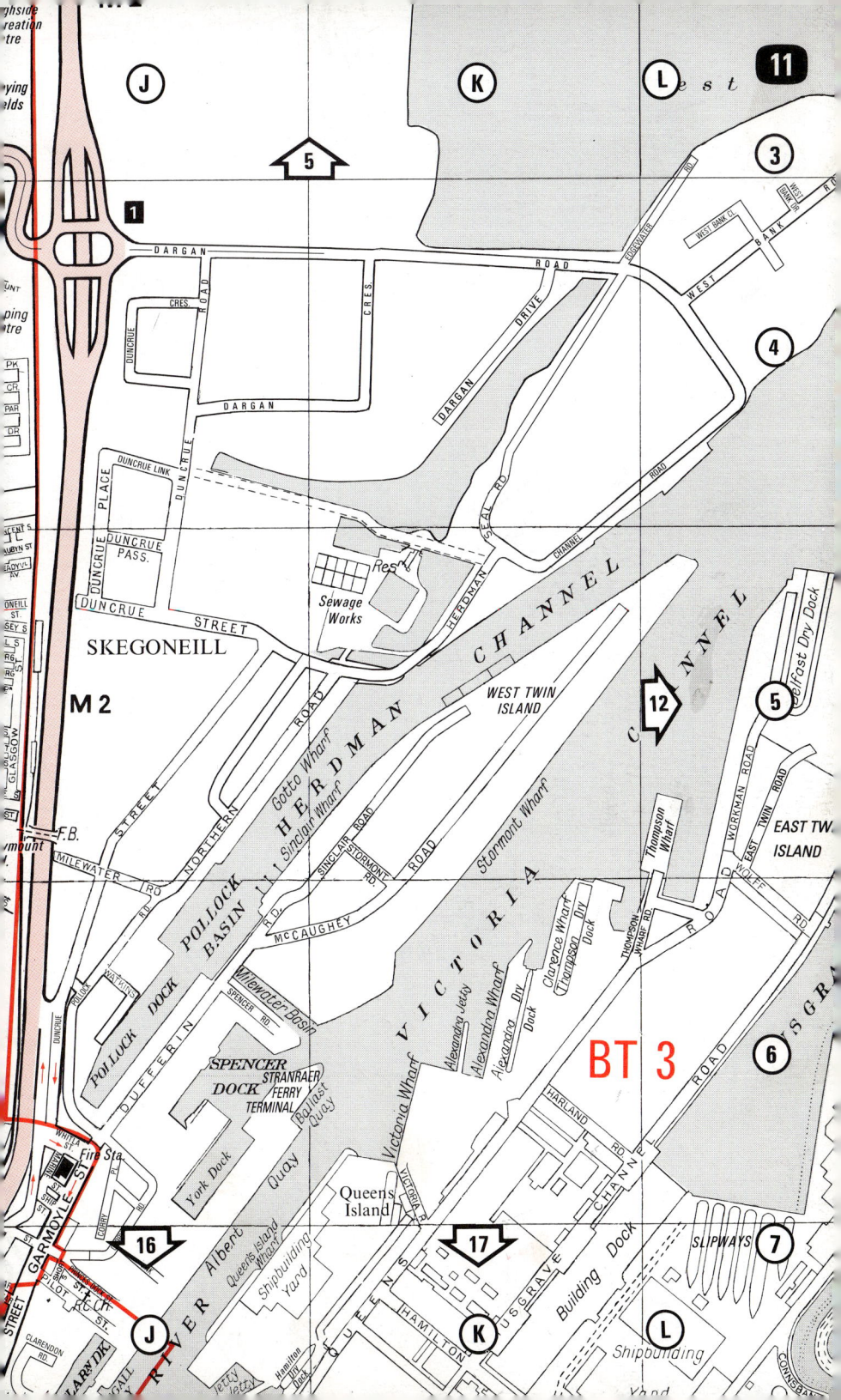

J   K   L est

5

1

DARGAN   ROAD

CRES.   DARGAN   CRES.

DUNCRUE   DARGAN   DRIVE

DARGAN

DUNCRUE LINK

DUNCRUE PLACE   DUNCRUE

SEAL RD.

3

4

WEST BANK RD.   WEST BANK C.   WEST BANK   WEST BANK RD.

EDGEWATER

WEST

DUNCRUE PASS.

DUNCRUE   STREET

Resⁿ

Sewage Works

HERDMAN   CHANNEL

CHANNEL

SKEGONEILL

M 2

WEST TWIN ISLAND

12   CHANNEL

Belfast Dry Dock

5

F.B.

MILEWATER   RO.

Gotto Wharf

Sinclair Wharf

HERDMAN   ROAD

Stormont Wharf

Thompson Wharf

WORKMAN   ROAD   EAST TWIN ROAD

EAST TW. ISLAND

STREET

NORTHERN   ROAD

SINCLAIR   STORMONT RD.

MCCAUGHEY

VICTORIA

Clarence Wharf   Thompson Dry Dock

Thompson Wharf RD.

WOLFF

ROAD

MUSGRAVE

6

POLLOCK   DOCK

POLLOCK BASIN   R.D.

Milewater Basin

SPENCER RD.

Alexandra Jetty   Alexandra Wharf   Alexandra Dry Dock

BT 3

WALNUT

POLLOCK

DUFFERIN

SPENCER DOCK   STRANRAER FERRY TERMINAL   Ballast Quay

Victoria Wharf   VICTORIA

HARLAND RD.

DUNCRUE

WHITLA ST.

Fire Sta.

York Dock

Albert   Queens Island Wharf

Queens Island

Shipbuilding Yard

QUEENS   HAMILTON

K

MUSGRAVE   CHANNEL

Building Dock

SLIPWAYS   7

L

GARMOYLE ST.

CORR   ST.   PILOT ST.

16

17

Shipbuilding Yard

CLARENDON RD.

J

RIVER

Queen's Quay

Jetty Jetty

Hamilton Dock

STREET   LARN DK.

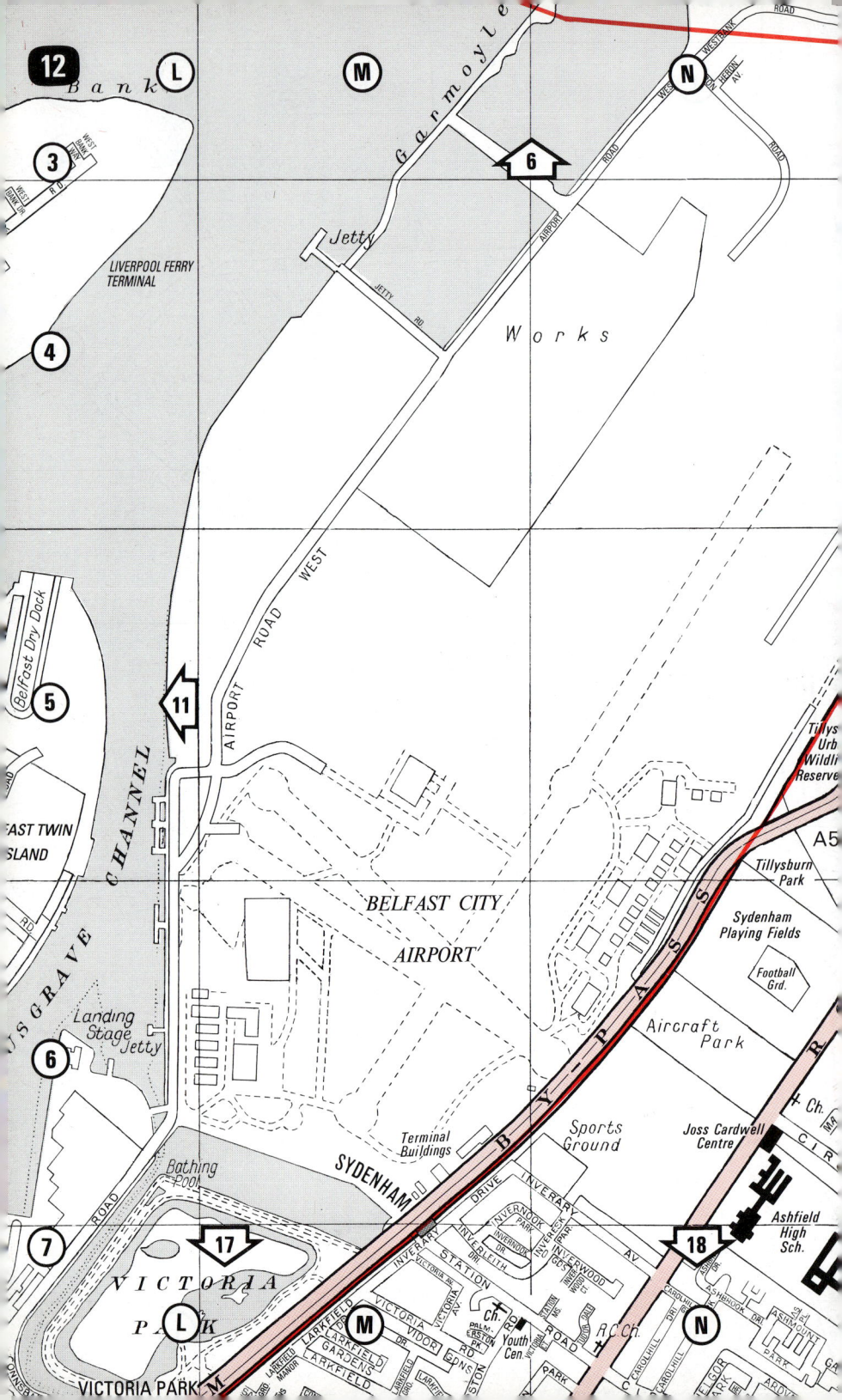

12

Bank

L

M

N

Garmoyle

WESTBANK

WEST BANK RD

ROAD

HERON AV

3

WEST BANK RD

6

Jetty

JETTY RD

Works

AIRPORT ROAD

LIVERPOOL FERRY
TERMINAL

4

Airport Road West

Belfast Dry Dock

5

11

Tillys
Urb
Wildli
Reserve

BELFAST TWIN
ISLAND

A5

Tillysburn
Park

MUSGRAVE CHANNEL

BELFAST CITY

AIRPORT

Sydenham
Playing Fields

Football
Grd.

Landing
Stage Jetty

6

Aircraft
Park

B Y - P A S S

Terminal
Buildings

Sports
Ground

Joss Cardwell
Centre

Ch.

CIR

Bathing
Pool

7

ROAD

SYDENHAM

INVERARY DRIVE

STATION

INVERWOOD
PARK

INVERARY AV

Ashfield
High
Sch.

17

18

N

VICTORIA

INVERLEITH DR

VICTORIA RD

DALM..
EASTON

Ch.
RD

Youth
Cen.

ROAD

R..ch.

PARK

L

M

N

PARK

LARKFIELD
MANOR

LARKFIELD
DR

LARKFIELD
GARDENS

VIDOR..

VICTORIA RD

GDNS

Ch.

CARROLHILL...

ASHFIELD

VICTORIA PARK M

LARKFIELD

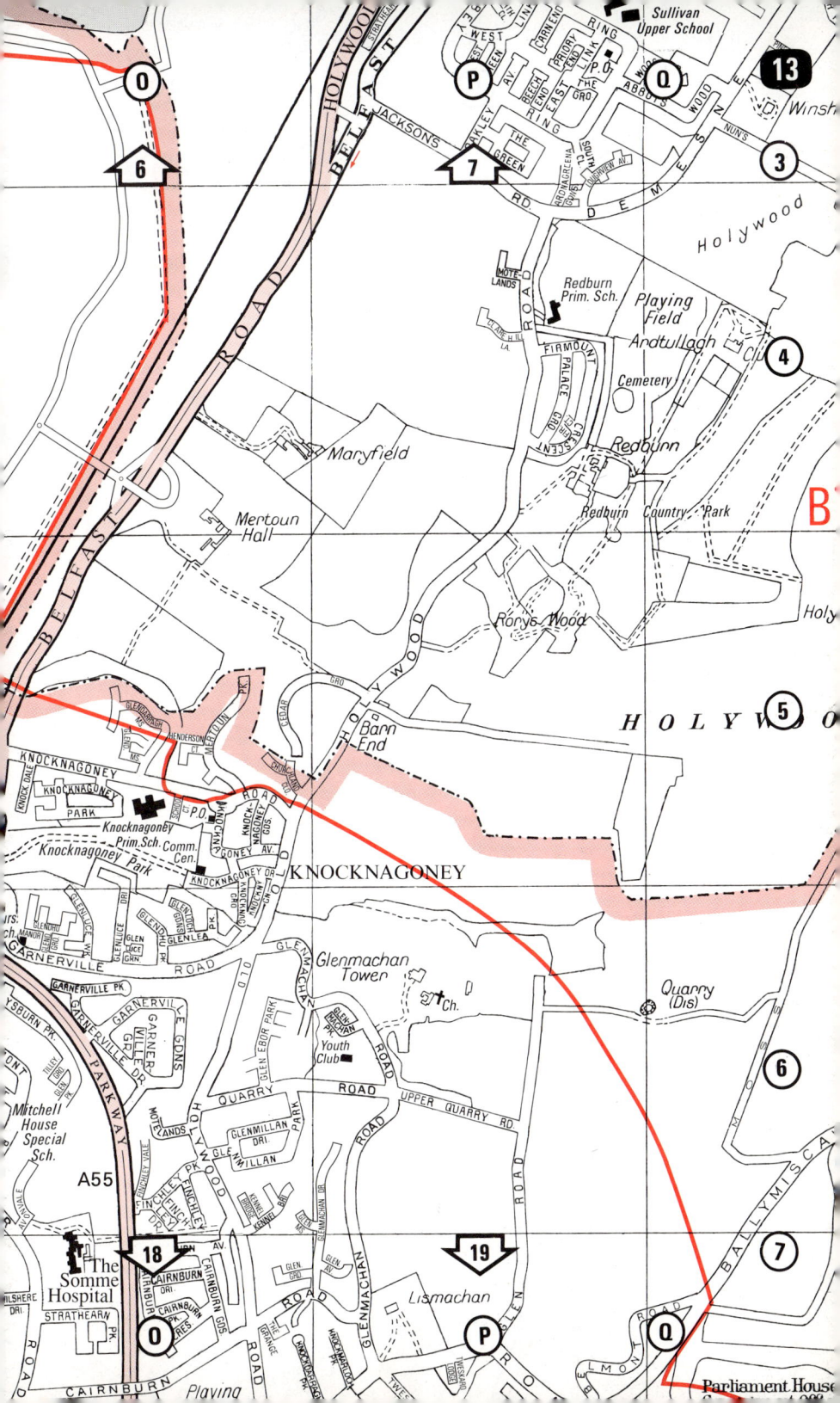

Sullivan Upper School

13

WEST
CARMEN
PRIORY RING LINK
GRO
ABBOTS WOOD
RING RD EAST
Winsh
P
Q

OAKLEY
THE GREEN
KILEY RD
NUN'S

3

Holywood

MOTE LANDS
Redburn Prim. Sch.
Playing Field
Andtullagh Clu

7

PALACE GRO
FIRMOUNT
CRESCENT

Cemetery

4

Maryfield

Redburn

Mertoun Hall

Redburn Country Park

B

Rorys Wood

HOLYWOOD

HOLY WOOD

GLENBURGH
Barn End
HENDERSON
MERTOUN PK

Knockdale

5

KNOCKNAGONEY PARK

Knocknagoney Prim.Sch. Comm. Cen.

Knock nagoney Park

KNOCKNAGONEY DR

CEDAR
SCHOOL
P.O.

KNOCK NAGONEY AV.

KNOCKNAGONEY ROAD

KNOCKNAGONEY

BELFAST ROAD

GARNERVILLE

GARNERVILLE PK
GARNERVILLE GDNS
GARNER VILLE DR

GLENMACHAN ROAD

GLEN EBOR PARK

Glenmachan Tower

Ch.

Youth Club

Quarry (Dis)

6

Mitchell House Special Sch.

A55

QUARRY
MOTE LANDS
GLENMILLAN DRI.
GLENWILLAN

PARK ROAD

UPPER QUARRY RD

QUARRY ROAD

GLEN ROAD

BALLYMISCA

The Somme Hospital

18

CAIRNBURN

FINCHLEY PK
FINCHLEY DRI.

KENNEL

CAIRNBURN DRI.

19

Lismachan

7

STRATHEARN

0

CAIRNBURN

Playing

P

Q

Parliament House

B C D

8 9

Glencairn Park

RIVER WAY

WESTWAY
WESTWAY GDNS
WESTWAY CRES
WESTWAY

R.C.A.

WESTWAY

Ch.

LYNDHURST
GDNS

LYNDHURST PK.
LYNDHURST GDS.

DUFFIELD

LYNDHURST
WAY
LYNDHURST
GRO
LYNDHURST
CLO
LYNDHURST
RISE

LYNDHURST PK.
LYND-
HURST
CLO

LYND. LA.

BALLY.
LA.

Mount
Gilbert
Community
College

ROAD

HIGHBURN
GDNS.

WEST

Loughview

Ballygomartin
Industrial Park

MOUNTAIN

Playing
Fields

Springhill
Prim.Sch.

Ch.

HIGHCLIFF GDS.
DENE
HIGH HILL
HIGHLANDZ Parade

HIGHVALE
GARDENS
HIGHCAIRN
GDNS.

HIGH
GDNS
HIGHPARK
CROSS

HIGHPARK
DRIVE
HIGH
LINK

HIGHCAIRN
DRIVE
HIGHGREEN

Comm.
Cen.

CIRCULAR

White Rock

White Rock
Quarry
(Dis)

BALLYGOMARTIN

Black
Mountain
Coll. & Prim.
Sch.

BALLYGOM.
WAY
BLK. MOUN.
WAY

SPRINGMARTIN ROAD

HIGHPARK
DRIVE
HIGHCAIRN

B. MT'N. GRD.
BLK. MT'N PL.

HIGH
PASS

R.U.C.
Sta.

ROAD

Whiterock

WHITEROCK

Quarry
(Dis)

Mill Race

ROAD

NEW BARNSLEY

MOYARD
CRES
MOYARD
PARADE

NEW BARNSLEY

MOYARD
PARK

SPRINGFIELD
PARK

SPRINGMARTIN
PK.
SPRINGFIELD

SPR. CRES.

B. MOUNTAIN

WAY

DRI.
DUNBOYNE

PRINGFIELD A55

BALLYMUR

NEW BARNSLEY
PK.
NEW BARNSLEY
GRO
NEW
GRO

Nurs.
Sch.

R.C.
Ch.

Vere Foster
Prim.Sch.

NEW
BARNSLEY
PARADE

NEW BARNSLEY

DIVISMORE

Girls'
Pr.Sch.

DIVISMORE PK.
DIVISMORE

SPRINGHILL
HEIGHTS

SPRINGHILL
GDNS

SPRINGHILL
HILL CRES

SPRINGHILL
GDNS.

WESTROCK
DRI.

WESTROCK
GRDS.

BRITTONS DRI.

DERMOTT HILL WAY
GARN'VILLE
HILL
DERMOTT
HILL

P.O.

ROAD

DIVISMORE
NEW

Gort Na Mona
Educational
Resource Centre

DERMOTT
PARK

DERMOTT
HILL

ALIVEN
PARK

St.Aidans
Prim.Sch.

Pr Sch.

Lib.
& Health
Centre

GLENALINA PK.
GLENALINA

BALLYMURPHY
CR.
BALLYMURPHY
DRI.

BALLY.
BALLYMURPHY
WHITECLIFF

BALLYMURPHY

SPRINGHILL

Ch.

WESTROCK
GDNS.

WHITEROCK GDNS.

WHITE

ROAD

Rockview
House

SPRINGFIELD

MONAGH

ROAD

NORGLEN
PAR

NORGLEN
PARK

ROAD

NORGLEN
DRIVE
NORGLEN
GRO

WH

AVENMORE PK.
AVON. AND
ARDMONAGH
GDNS.

DIVIS.
LEACH

BELFA'ST

Leisure
Centre

Corrigan
Park

Whiterock
Further Education
Centre

CEMETER

BRITTONS
PAR.

MONAGH
LINK
MONAGH
GRO

MONAGH ROAD

NORGLEN
DRIVE

ISAGH
MONAGH
GRO

NORGLEN
GRO

TURF LODGE

Swimming
Pool

FALLS

Pav.

PARK

Holy
Trinity Prim.
Schs.

NORGLEN
GDNS

NORFOLK
ROAD

NORFOLK
GDNS.

NORFOLK
GDNS
GREEN

NORFOLK
PARA.
NORBURY

DIVIS

Tennis
Grds.

20 21

Woodlands

MONAGH
LINK

B C D

St.Patricks
Training Sch.

A55

Ch.

GRANSHA
GDNS

UPTON
COTTS

UPTON
PARK

UPTON
GREEN

NORBURY
DRIVE

ROAD

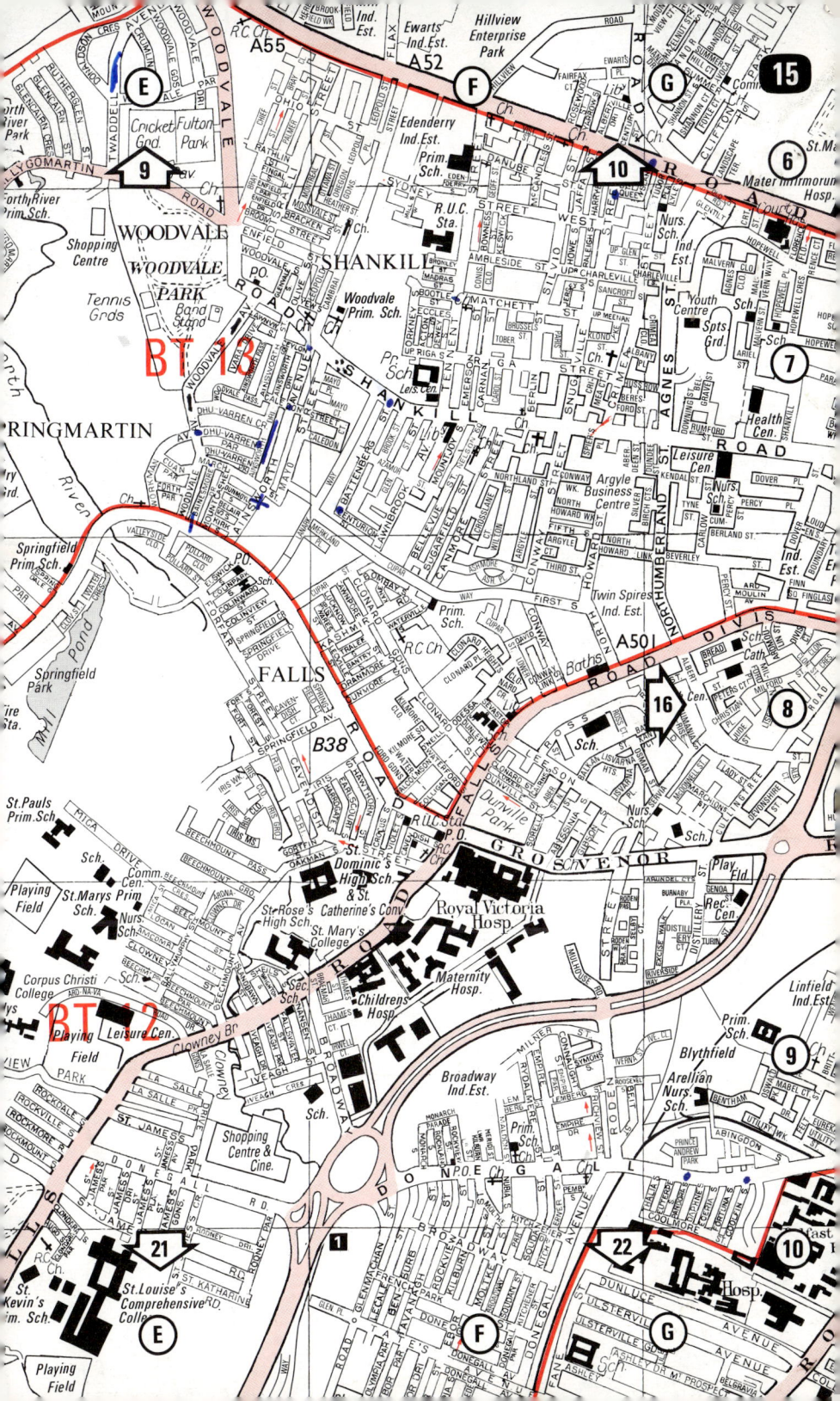

15

BT 13

BT 12

WOODVALE

WOODVALE PARK

SHANKILL

FALLS

RINGMARTIN

A55   A52

Cricket Grd.   Fulton Park

Shopping Centre

Tennis Grds   Band Stand

Woodvale Prim. Sch.

Forth River Park   Forth River Prim. Sch.

Ewarts Ind. Est.   Hillview Enterprise Park

Edenderry Ind. Est.   Prim. Sch.   Eden Derry

R.U.C. Sta.   R.U.C. Sta.

Youth Centre   Spts Grd

Health Cen.

Mater Infirmorum Hosp.

Leisure Cen.   Argyle Business Centre

Twin Spires Ind. Est.

A501   ROAD   DIVIS

Springfield Prim. Sch.

Springfield Park

Mill Pond

St. Pauls Prim. Sch.

Dunville Park

B38

Baths

GROSVENOR   ROAD

St. Dominic's High Sch.   St. Catherine's Conv.

St. Rose's High Sch.   St. Mary's College

Royal Victoria Hosp.

Maternity Hosp.

Childrens Hosp.

St. Marys Prim Sch.   Nurs. Sch.

Corpus Christi College

Playing Field

Leisure Cen.

BROADWAY

Broadway Ind. Est.

Shopping Centre & Cine.

St. James'

Linfield Ind. Est.

Prim. Sch.

Blythfield

Arellian Nurs. Sch.

Prince Andrew Park

St. Louise's Comprehensive College

St. Kevin's Prim. Sch.

Playing Field

DONEGALL   ROAD

ULSTERVILLE   AVENUE

Hosp.

SHANKILL ROAD   WOODVALE ROAD   SPRINGFIELD ROAD   FALLS ROAD   GROSVENOR ROAD   AGNES ST   NORTHUMBERLAND ST

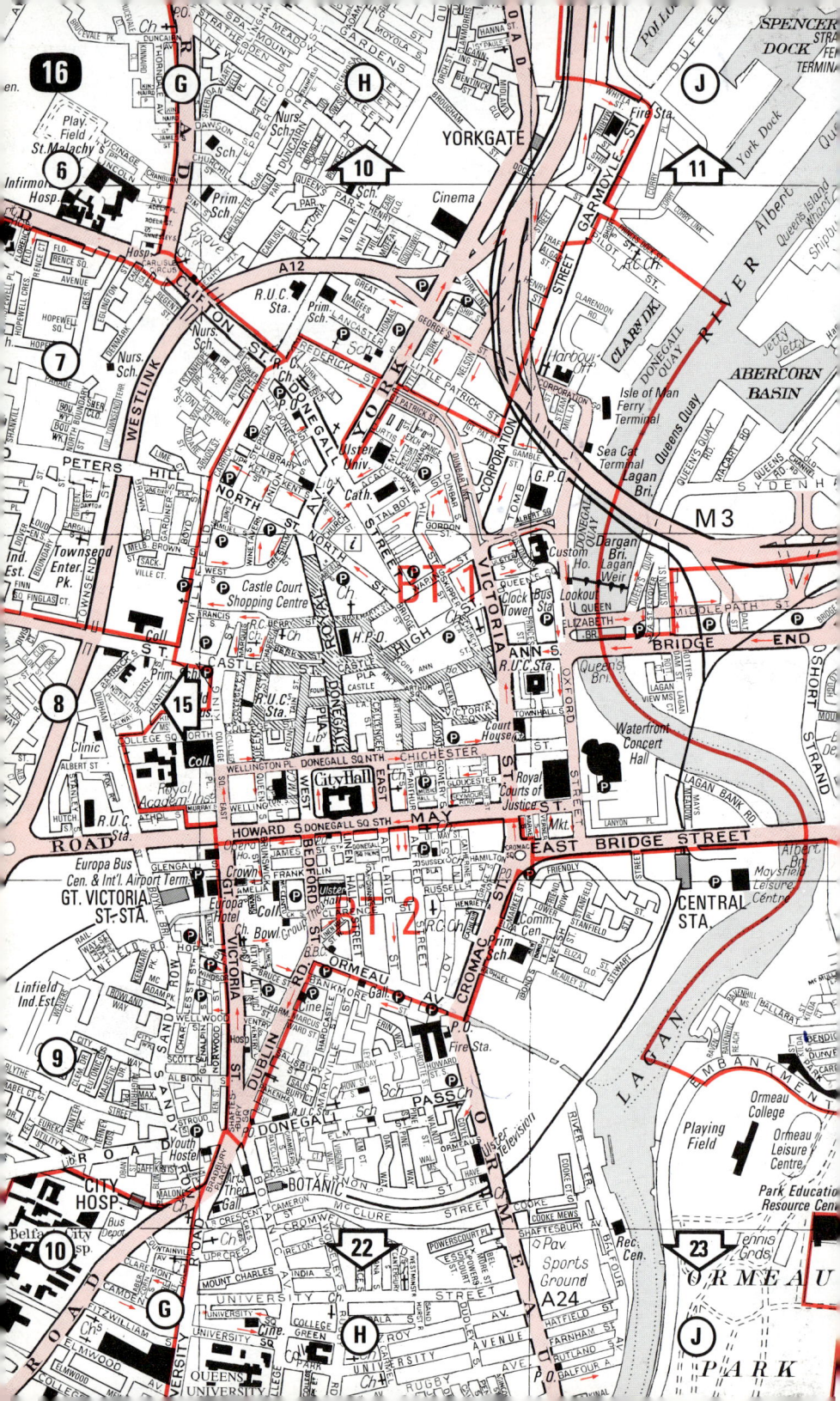

SPENCER DOCK

YORKGATE

RIVER LAGAN

ABERCORN BASIN

M 3

Queen's Quay

Donegall Quay

Isle of Man Ferry Terminal

Sea Cat Terminal

Custom Ho.

G.P.O.

Clarendon Dock

Ulster Univ.

Cath.

Castle Court Shopping Centre

St. Malachy's Play. Field

Infirm^l Hosp.

PETERS HILL

Townsend Enter. Pk.

Ind. Est.

R.U.C. Sta.

Royal Academ^l Inst

City Hall

DONEGALL SQUARE

Wellington Pl.

Howard S^t

Chichester St.

Royal Courts of Justice

Court House

R.U.C. Sta.

Waterfront Concert Hall

BRIDGE END

O'SHORT STRAND

MIDDLEPATH ST.

SYDENHAM

Queen Elizabeth Br.

Queen's Br.

Lagan Weir

Dargan Br.

Clock Tower

Bus Sta.

Lookout

Europa Bus Cen. & Int'l. Airport Term.

GT. VICTORIA ST. STA.

Europa Hotel

Crown

Central Sta.

EAST BRIDGE STREET

Maysfield Leisure Centre

Albert Br.

Ulster Television

Fire Sta.

Youth Hostel

CITY HOSP.

City Bus Depot

Ormeau College

Ormeau Leisure Centre

Playing Field

Park Education Resource Cen.

BOTANIC

QUEENS UNIVERSITY

ORMEAU PARK

A24

A12

BT1

BT2

Linfield Ind. Est.

DONEGALL PASS

DUBLIN RD

ORMEAU RD

Sports Ground

Pav

Rec. Cen.

Tennis Grnds

LAGAN BANK RD

EMBANKMENT

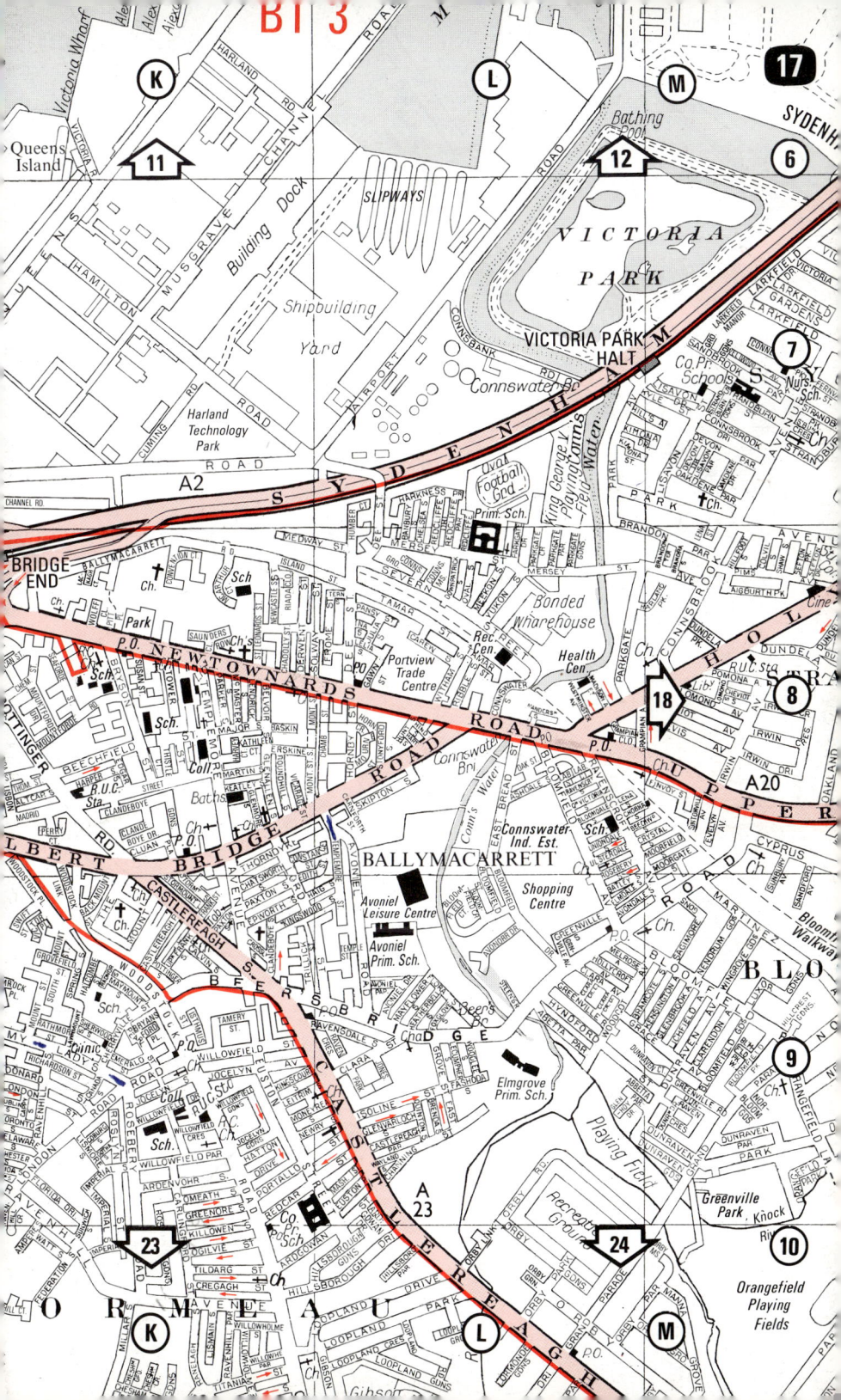

K L M

SYDENH

Queens
Island

11 12 6

Bathing
Pool

SLIPWAYS

VICTORIA

Building Dock

PARK

Shipbuilding
Yard

VICTORIA PARK
HALT

Connsbank

Connswater Rd

Co. Pr. Schools

Harland
Technology
Park

LARKFIELD
LARKFIELD
GARDENS
LARKFIELD

Nurs.
Sch.

7

A2

CHANNEL RD.

S Y D E N H A M

King George V
Playing Fields

BRIDGE
END

BALLYMACARRETT

Ch.

Sch.

Harkness Dr.

Prim. Sch.

Bonded
Wharehouse

Health
Cen.

Co. Pr. Sch.

8

Park

P.O. N E W T O W N A R D S

Portview
Trade Centre

Rec.
Cen.

18

ROAD

A20

U P P E R

Beechfield

R.U.C.
Sta.

Sch.

Coll.

Connswater
Bri.

Connswater
Ind. Est.

Sch.

CYPRUS

Bloom
Walkwa

BLO

A L B E R T   B R I D G E   R O A D

BALLYMACARRETT

Shopping
Centre

Avoniel
Leisure Centre

Avoniel
Prim. Sch.

CASTLEREAGH

Ch.

Elmgrove
Prim. Sch.

9

Clinic

Coll.

Sch.

R.C.

Playing Field

Greenville
Park Knock

10

23 24

A23

Co.
Pr.
Sch.

Recreation
Ground

Orangefield
Playing
Fields

O R M E A U

K L M

P.O.

18

Terminal Buildings

M

Sports Ground

N Cardwell Centre

O

QUARRY

GLENMILLAN DRI

SYDENHAM

6

CIRCULAR

MARMONT CR.

Ch.

Mitchell House Special Sch.

A55

13

INVERARY

DRIVE

STATION

12

Ashfield High Sch.

CAIRNBURN AV.

CAIRNBURN

CAIRNBURN DRI

CAIRNBURN PK

CAIRNBURN CRES

CAIRNBURN GDS

INVERNOOK PARK

INVERNOOK

INVELEITH

INTERWOOD

The Somme Hospital

STRATHEARN

ROAD

CAIRNBURN ROAD

Playing Fields

VICTORIA

VIDOR

ROAD

Ch.

Youth Cen.

R.C.Ch.

WILSHERE DRI

ASHMOUNT PARK

GARRANARD PARK

BT 4

Belmont Park

7

PALMERSTON

CLONAVER

CLONAVER GDS

CLONAVER DR

NORWOOD

AVENUE

DRIVE

C.I.Y.M.S. Sports Ground

Play Field

BELM

SCHOMBERG AV.

SCHOMBERG PARK

HAWTHORNDEN

SYDENHAM

CRES

SYDENHAM GDS

EDGECUMBE VIEW

EDGECUMBE DR

NORWOOD CR

NORWOOD PK

Strathearn School Belavon

SNOW

CLONALLON PK.

THE CAIRNS

Ch.

LAUREL-VALE

WANDSWORTH

PEMBROKE

HAWTH'DEN GDS

ROAD

VENUE

Cine

DUNDELA

B.P.

EDEN

CLONALLON

CLONALLON CT.

BELMONT

WANDSWORTH DRI

Ormiston

HAWTHORNDEN WAY

STRANDTOWN

8

DUNDELA

WILGAR

Dundela Inf Sch.

Fire Sta.

17

EARLS WOOD RD.

EARLSWOOD ROAD

Belmont Prim. Sch. P.O.

CAMPBELL

BELMONT

Belmont Prim. Sch.

Tennis Gdns

Strandtown Prim.Sch.

Pav.

KINCORA

Bowling Grn

EASTLEIGH

HUSS

WANDS

BELMONT

KNOCKLOFTY PARK

THE HAMLETS

OAKLAND

Spec. Sch.

ORMISTON PARK

ORMISTON

R

GREENWOOD AV

Prim. Sch.

Lib.

NEWTOWNARD

KNOCKDENE PK NORTH

Ch

BLOOMFIELD

CYPRUS PARK

PRIM. SCH

CRES

HOUSTON

TEWITT PARK

R.C. Ch.

ENID PK

ENID PARADE

Bloomfield Coll Sch

WINSTON GDNS

ORMISTON GDNS

GREEN CR

P.O.

KNOCK-DENE PARK

BLOOMFIELD Walkway

Bloomfield

HOLLAND PK

HOLLAND GDNS

BALLYHACKAMORE

Coll PARK

SANDOWN DRI

KINGS

GREEN

KNOCKDENE

9

ORANGEFIELD

Beersbridge Nature Walk

KIRKLISTON PARK

SANDOWN PK

ASTORIA GDNS

Ch

Sandown

Brooklyn

KINGS

A55

R.U.C. Sta.

CHERRYVALLEY

ROAD

ORANGEFIELD GDNS

ORANGEFIELD AV

SANDHILL

ROAD

SANDHILL GDS

KNOCK-VALE GRO

KNOCK

KINGS CRES

CHERRYVALLEY

Mill Pond

CLARA

NEILL'S HILL

CLARA WAY

RICHHILL

KNOCK-CASTLE PK

KENSINGTON

BT 5

10

24

Sports Ground

HILL CRESCENT

Knock Burial Ground

SHANDON

25

M Orangefield h Sch.

Sports Grounds

N

KNOCK

O

P Q R

6

UPPER QUA...

ROAD

GLEN ROAD

MASSEY ROAD

Lismachan

Kileen House

Castle View

7

13

BALLYMISCW

BELMONT ROAD

WESTKARD PARK

MASSEY PARK

CLOVERHILL PK.

Netherleigh

AVENUE

CASTLEHILL MANOR

CASTLEHILL DR.

CASTLEHILL PK.

Parliament House & Government Offices

Stormont Castle

Speaker's House

R.U.C. Sta.

8

Playing Fields

CASTLEHILL PK. WEST

STORMONT PARK

PRINCE OF WALES AVENUE

Ministry of Agriculture Research Stations

Cabin Hill

Ch.

The Maynard Sinclair Pavilion

Pav.

Playing Fields Pav.

Playing Fields

Dundonald House

Knock Golf Course

Summerfield

DUN

A20

ROAD

STORMONT CT.

P.O.

Ch.

ROSEMOUNT

ROSEPARK

ROSEPARK EAST

ROSEPARK CENT

ROSEPARK S

Rose Park

ARDCARN

DUNDONALD

THORNHILL DR.

KNOCKBN PK.

CASTLEVIEW RD.

THORNHILL

SUMMERHILL PARK

SUMMERHILL

CLOGHAN

ROAD

KNOCKLAND PARK

Gravel Pit

ARDCARN GRN.

ARDCARN DR.

CEMETERY

9

CABIN HILL PK

THORNHILL PDE.

THORNHILL PARK

BARNETT'S

ABBEY GDNS.

Knock River

ABBEY

PARK

ABBEY

Hazelbank

KINGSDALE PARK

GORTIN PARK

ABBEY

ROAD

KINGS BRAE

Nth SPERRIN

5th SPERRIN

SPERRIN DR.

SPERRIN PK.

KINROSS

Lib.

DALRY PARK

KINROSS AV.

AVENUE

BT 16

GILNAHIRK

P.O.

KINGS SQ.

TULLYCARNET

KINGS

KINGSWAY PARK

KINGSWAY LINN

KINGSLAND DR

KINGSLAND

GRANTON PK.

P.O.

ROAD

OLD DUNDONAL

Playing Field

KINGSWAY AV.

KINGSWAY

25

FORT DRIVE

KINGS ...

ROSLIN

MELFORT DRIVE

LOWLAND AV.

LOTHIAN AV.

CHINVER DRIVE

LEVEN CRES.

RISE

VIONVILLE

Sch.

Beech Hill

Hanwood House

10

Dundon Internat Ice Bo

Playing Fields

Our Lady & St Patricks Ill.

Gilnahirk Prim. Sch.

Tullycarnet Park

P Q R

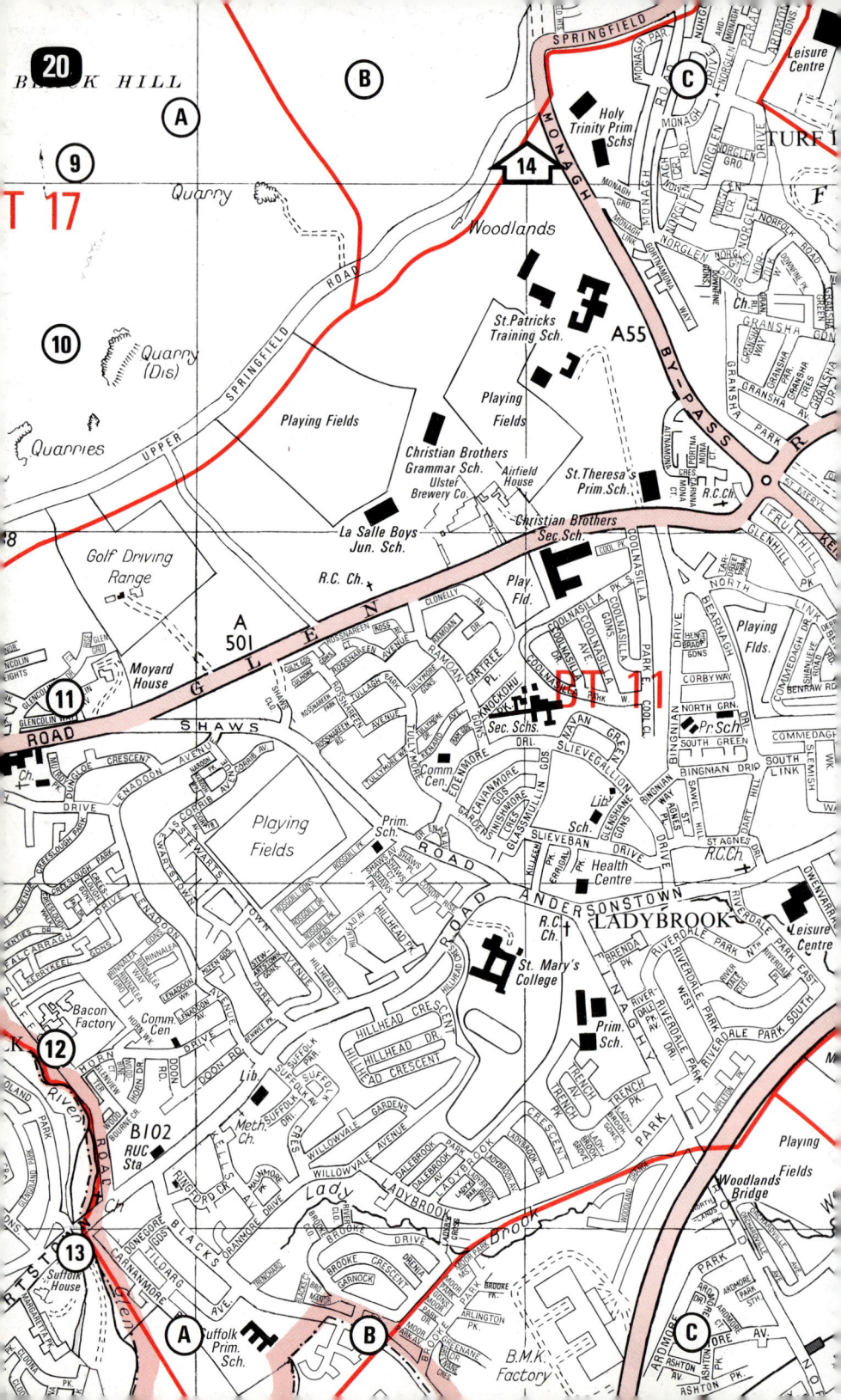

BLACK HILL

T 17

20

A
B
C
9
10
11
12
13

Quarry

Quarry (Dis)

Quarries

SPRINGFIELD ROAD

UPPER SPRINGFIELD ROAD

Golf Driving Range

Moyard House

A 501

GLEN ROAD

SHAWS ROAD

Playing Fields

Ch.

Bacon Factory

Comm Cen

Lib.

Meth. Ch.

B102

RUC Sta.

Suffolk House

Suffolk Prim. Sch.

A
B
C

Woodlands

St.Patricks Training Sch.

A55

Playing Fields

Christian Brothers Grammar Sch.
Ulster Brewery Co.

La Salle Boys Jun. Sch.

R.C. Ch.

Airfield House

Christian Brothers Sec.Sch.

St.Theresa's Prim.Sch.

Play. Fld.

R.C.Ch.

BT 11

Sec. Schs.

Prim. Sch.

Comm. Cen.

Prim. Sch.

St. Mary's College

R.C. Ch.

Prim. Sch.

ANDERSONSTOWN ROAD

LADYBROOK

Health Centre

Lib. Sch.

St Agnes Ch.
R.C.Ch.

Pr.Sch.

Playing Flds.

Leisure Centre

Health Centre

Holy Trinity Prim Schs

14

MONAGH BY-PASS

MONAGH ROAD

TURF

Leisure Centre

Hillhead Crescent

Willowvale Avenue

Willowvale Gardens

Ladybrook

B.M.K. Factory

Woodlands Bridge

Playing Fields

Lady Brook

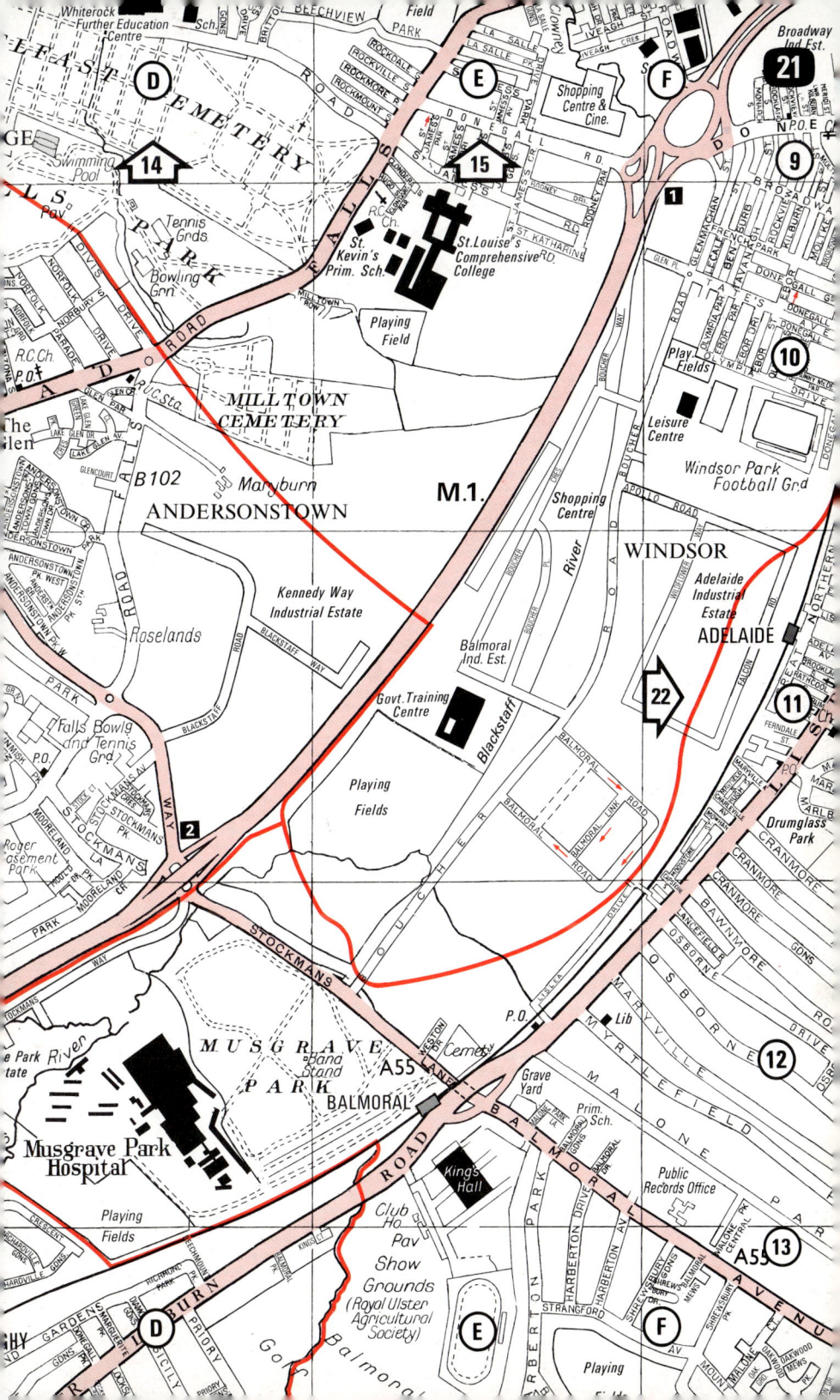

Whiterock Further Education Centre

BLECHVIEW Field

Broadway Ind Est

21

Sch.

CEMETERY

D

Swimming Pool

ROCKDALE
ROCKVILLE S
ROCKMORE
ROCKMOUNT

LA SALLE
LA SALLE PK
DONEGALL

Shopping Centre & Cine.

VEAGH

E

F

1

9

FALLS PARK

Tennis Grds

Bowling Grn

St. Kevin's Prim. Sch.

St. Louise's Comprehensive College

14

15

GLENCHAN
OLYMPIA PK
OLYMPIA DR
DONEGALL
DONEGALL

10

Norfolk

R.C.Ch.
P.O

MILLTOWN CEMETERY

Maryburn

B 102

ANDERSONSTOWN

Playing Field

M.1.

Shopping Centre

Leisure Centre

Windsor Park Football Grd

WINDSOR

Roselands

Kennedy Way Industrial Estate

Adelaide Industrial Estate

ADELAIDE

22

11

Falls Bowlg and Tennis Grd

Roger Casement Park

STOCKMANS

Blackstaff Way

Govt. Training Centre

Balmoral Ind. Est.

Playing Fields

Blackstaff

Balmoral LINK ROAD

Drumglass Park

CRANMORE

2

STOCKMANS

Park River state

MUSGRAVE PARK

Band Stand

A55

BALMORAL

Cemet

P.O.
Lib

Grave Yard

Prim. Sch.

Public Records Office

MALONE

MYRTLEFIELD

OSBORNE

12

Musgrave Park Hospital

Playing Fields

Kings Hall

Club Ho.

Pav

Show Grounds
(Royal Ulster Agricultural Society)

A55 AVENUE

13

D

E

F

Playing

Golf

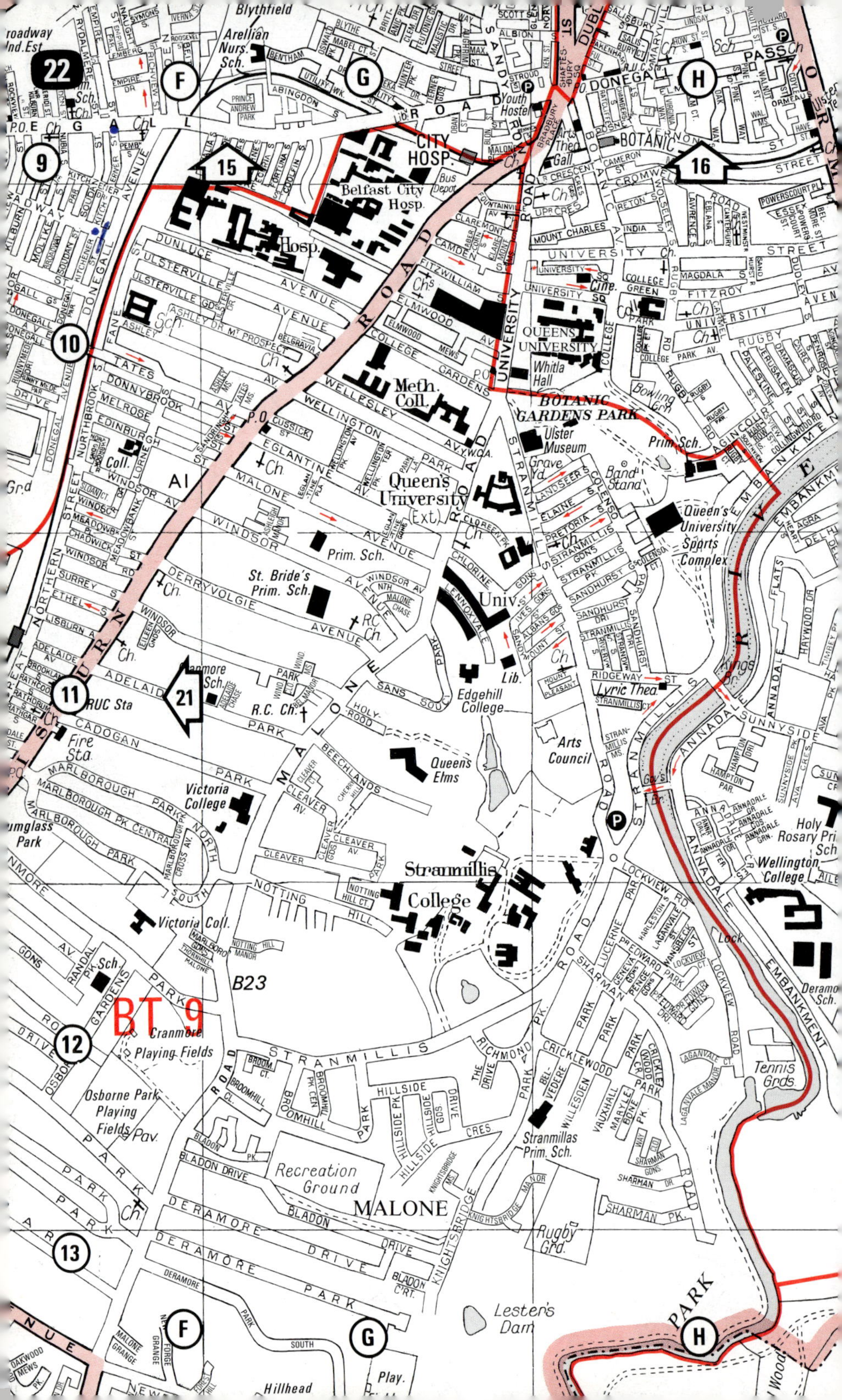

22
F
G
H
9
10
11
12
13
15
16
21
Blythfield
Arellian Nurs. Sch.
Broadway Ind. Est
DONEGALL ROAD
SANDY ROW
DUBLIN ROAD
Youth Hostel
CITY HOSP.
Belfast City Hosp.
Hosp.
Bus Depot
Arts Theatre Gall
BOTANIC
DONEGALL PASS
UNIVERSITY STREET
LISBURN ROAD
DUNLUCE AVENUE
ULSTERVILLE AVENUE
ASHLEY AVENUE
TATES AVENUE
DONNYBROOK
MELROSE
EDINBURGH
WINDSOR AVENUE
DERRYVOLGIE AVENUE
ADELAIDE PARK
CADOGAN PARK
MARLBOROUGH PARK
MALONE ROAD
ELMWOOD AVENUE
COLLEGE GARDENS
WELLESLEY AVENUE
WELLINGTON PARK
EGLANTINE AVENUE
Queen's University (Ext)
QUEENS UNIVERSITY
Whitla Hall
Meth. Coll.
BOTANIC GARDENS PARK
Ulster Museum
Band Stand
Prim Sch.
Queen's University Sports Complex
STRANMILLIS ROAD
Edgehill College
Lib.
Lyric Thea.
Arts Council
Queens Elms
Victoria College
Victoria Coll.
Stranmillis College
St. Bride's Prim. Sch.
Prim. Sch.
R.C. Ch.
RUC Sta
Fire Sta
Cranmore Sch.
BT 9
B23
Cranmore Playing Fields
Osborne Park Playing Fields Pav.
Recreation Ground
MALONE
STRANMILLIS ROAD
Stranmillas Prim. Sch.
Rugby Grd.
Lester's Dam
DERAMORE DRIVE
DERAMORE PARK
BLADON DRIVE
KNIGHTSBRIDGE
SHARMAN ROAD
LOCKVIEW ROAD
EMBANKMENT
ANNADALE
Kings Br.
Gov's Br.
Holy Rosary Prim Sch
Wellington College
Deramore Sch.
Tennis Grds.
Lock
RIVER LAGAN
Hillhead
Play.

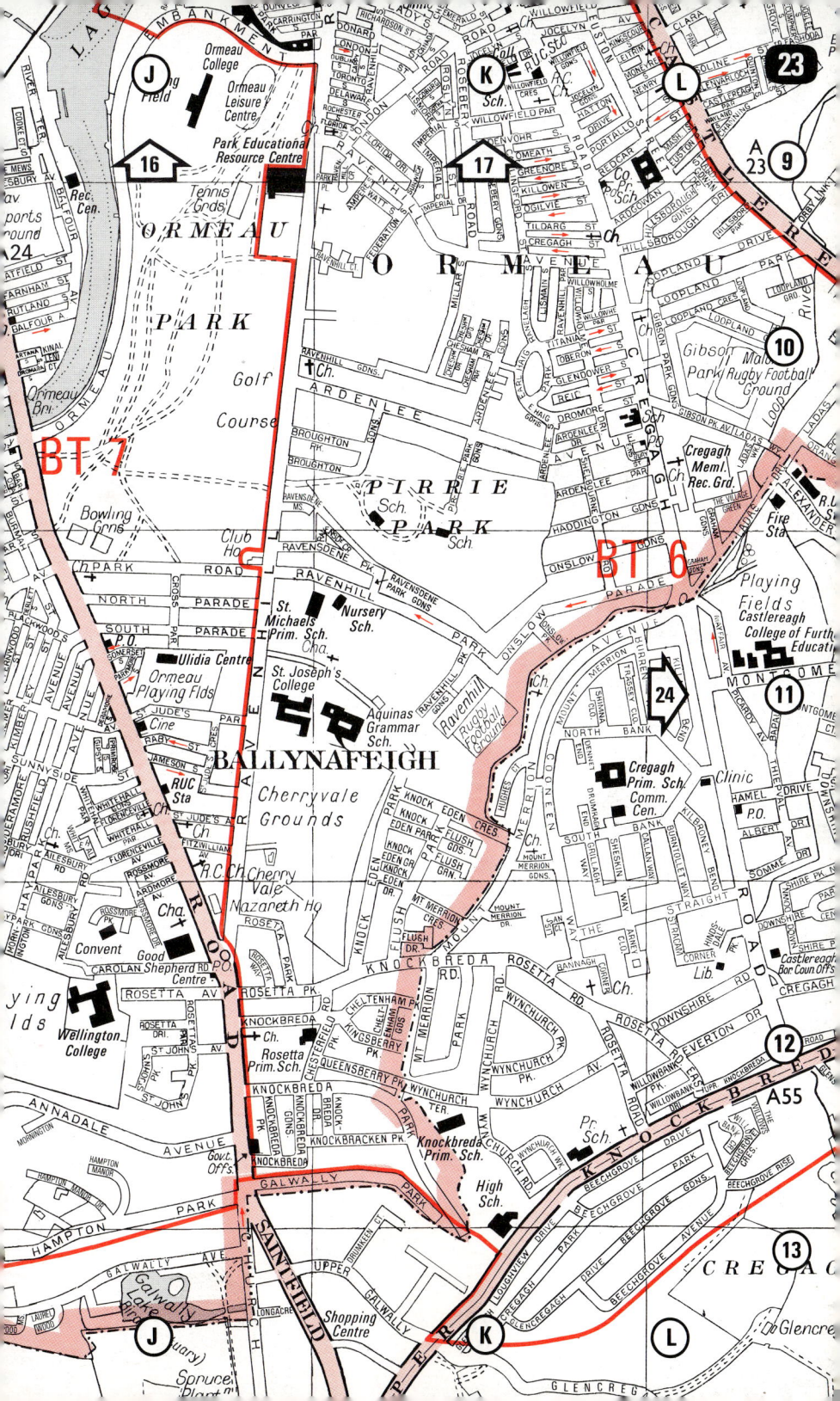

J

Ormeau College

ng Field

Ormeau Leisure Centre

Park Educational Resource Centre

16

Tennis Grds

O R M E A U

P A R K

Golf Course

BT 7

Bowling Gns

Rec. Cen.

ports ound

24

Ormeau Bri.

Club Ho.

Ravensdene Pk

ARDENLEE

BROUGHTON PK.

BROUGHTON

P I R R I E   P A R K

Sch.

Sch.

Ch Park

Road

RAVENHILL

NORTH   PARADE

SOUTH   PARADE

St. Michaels Prim. Sch.

Nursery Sch.

Ravensdene Park Gdns

Ch.

Ulidia Centre

Ormeau Playing Flds

P.O.

St. Joseph's College

Jude's Cine

Aquinas Grammar Sch.

RUC Sta

BALLYNAFEIGH

Cherryvale Grounds

Jameson St

Whitehall

Florenceville Av.

Rossmore Av.

 Rby St

Jude's Av

Ch

Fitzwilliam

R.C.Ch

Cherry Vale

Nazareth Ho.

Convent

Good Shepherd Centre

CAROLAN

ROSETTA AV.

Rosetta Av.

KNOCKBREDA

Ch.

Rosetta Prim. Sch.

KNOCKBREDA

St John's

Wellington College

Chesterfield

Kingsberry Pk.

Queensberry Pk.

ANNADALE

AVENUE

Govt. Offs.

GALWALLY

HAMPTON

SAINTFIELD

GALWALLY

UPPER GALWALLY

Galwally Lake (uary)

Shopping Centre

Spruce Plant

LONGACRE

J

K

Sch.

WILLOWFIELD

Coll

JOCELYN

K

Sch.

WILLOWFIELD CRES

WILLOWFIELD PAR

Co. Prim. Sch.

RAVENHILL ROAD

17

O R M E A U

OMEATH

GREENORE

KILLOWEN

OGILVIE

TILDARG ST

CREGAGH

Ch.

AVENUE

WILLOWHOLME

ARDENLEE

AVENUE

HADDINGTON GDNS

DROMORE

ARDENLEE DRIVE

ARDENLEE GDNS

ONSLOW   PARADE

Ch.

Ravenhill Rugby Football Ground

KNOCK EDEN CRES

KNOCK EDEN PARK

FLUSH GDS

FLUSH GRN.

KNOCK EDEN GR.

KNOCK EDEN DR.

MT. MERRION CRES

MOUNT MERRION DR.

FLUSH DR.

MT. MERRION AV.

KNOCKBREDA RD.

ROSETTA RD.

HELTENHAM PK.

WYNCHURCH RD.

WYNCHURCH

WYNCHURCH PK.

WYNCHURCH

Knockbreda Prim. Sch.

KNOCKBRACKEN PK.

High Sch.

CHURCH RD.

L

A 23

9

HILLSBOROUGH   DRIVE

LOOPLAND PARK

LOOPLAND GRO.

LOOPLAND DRIVE

Gibson Park Rugby Football Ground

Maid

10

GIBSON PK. AV

LADAS

Cregagh Meml. Rec. Grd.

BT 6

The Village Green

Fire Sta

ALEXANDER

R.U.

Playing Fields

Castlereagh College of Furth Educati

11

MONTGOMERY

Cregagh Prim. Sch. Comm. Cen.

24

NORTH BANK

SOUTH BANK

Clinic

HAMEL DRIVE

P.O.

ALBERT

Castlereagh Bor Coun Offs

Lib.

CREGAGH

THE

CORNER

SHESKIN

STRAIGHT

Downsview

ROSETTA

EVERTON DR.

WILLOWBANK

12

A55

Pr. Sch.

KNOCKBREDA

BEECHGROVE PARK

BEECHGROVE GDNS

BEECHGROVE AVENUE

BEECHGROVE RISE

13

C R E G A G

K

L

Dr Glencre

GLENCREG

23

Elmgrove Sch.

L M N

9 Greenville Park

17 18

Playing Field

Recreation Ground

Knock River

Orangefield Playing Fields

Orangefield High Sch.

Sports Ground

Sports Grounds

Grosvenor Grammar Sch.

Pr. Sch.

Playing Fields

10 P.O.

Sports Grd.

Orangefield

R.U.C. Sta.

Ch.

Castleregh Ind. Est.

CASTLEREAGH

Alanbrooke Park Ind. Est.

Castleregh College of Further Education

Clinic & Lib.

Roddens Cres.

Roddens Park

Roddens Gdns.

Roddens Cres.

11 23

The Robinson Centre Comm. Cen.

Carnamena Nurs. Sch.

Carnamena Gds.

Clonduff

High Sch.

Prim. Sch.

Glensharragh Pr. Sch.

P.O.

Lisnasharragh Pk.

Casaeldona Park

Casaeldona Cres.

Casaeldona Av.

Prim. Sch.

Crawford Pk.

Rosemount Pk.

Glenview Gdns.

Glenview Avenue

Glenview Cres.

Glenview

Castlemore Castlemont Pk.

Delamont Pk.

Marlborough Heights

Grey Castle Manor

CREGAGH

12

astlereagh Coun Off's.

Ch.

Playing Fields

Beechmount

Castlereagh

Ch.

Grave Yard

Castleregh House

13 HILLS

Cregagh Hill

Charleville

L M N

Glencregagh

Blooming

Castlereagh

Slata House

Mos Cotta

A55

Brooklyn

O

CK

CT 5

18

KINGS CRES
KINGSDALE
PARK
BARNET ROAD
HAZELBANK
KINGS DRI
KINGS SQ
P.O.
P
TULLYCARNET
KINGS
KINGSWAY AV.
ABBEY
Q
NTH SPERRIN
SPERRIN
SPERRIN DR.
SPERRIN PK.
P.O.
Lib.
GRAN

9

CHERRY VALLEY
KENSINGTON
SHANDON
KENSINGTON GDNS
KENSINGTON DRI.
KINGSWAY
19
KINGSWAY PARK
KINGSLAND DR
KINGSLAND DR
MELFORT DRIVE
MELFORT PK.
ROSLIN
LOTHIA
10

SHANDON PARK
KENSINGTON ROAD
CHURCHFIELD
GILNAHIRK ROAD
Gilnahirk Park
Playing Fields
Our Lady & St. Patricks Coll.
Gilnahirk Prim. Sch.
HELENS LEA
Tullycarnet Park
GEARY RD
MOYNE RD
RUSSELL PK
KILMAKEE PK.
BRISTOW PK.

Shandon Park
Club Ho.

Golf Course

GILNAHIRK DRI.
GILNAHIRK
GILNAHIRK AV.
GILNAHIRK WALK
GILNAHIRK RISE
BRIARWOOD PARK
BROOK MEADOW
Clinic & Lib.
GORTLAND
PARK
CHARTERS AV.
Ch.
Ch.
GILNAHIRK ROAD

BRANIEL

DRIVE
MARLFIELD
MARLFIELD
FARMHURST
FARM HURST WAY
GREEN
FARMHURST
WOODVIEW PK. W.
WOODVIEW DRI.
ALTA
AVENUE
CREEVY
GROVE
WARREN PARK GDS
FAIRWAY GDS.
Comm. Cen.
Ch.
WOODVIEW DRI.

GILNAHIRK

Rockmount House

11

SOUTHLAND DALE
RAVENSWOOD
Co.Pr.Sch.
BRANIEL
WOODCROFT HEIGHTS
WOODCROFT RISE
SHAN. HTS.

GILNAHIRK ROAD WEST
BALLYHANWOOD

Quarry (Dis)

Braniel Hill

C A S T L E R E A G H

Mann's Corner

MIDDLE BRANIEL ROAD

MANN

12

Rockvale
Playing Field

BRANIEL ROAD
UPPER BRANIEL ROAD
LISLEA
MANN RD

Ashgrove

Meahangs Hill

Scrabo View

Meahargs Thorn

13

23

O

P

Q

INDEX TO STREETS

General Abbreviations

All.	Alley	Ct.	Court	Lo.	Lodge	S.	South
Arc.	Arcade	Cts	Courts	Lwr.	Lower	Sq.	Square
Av.	Avenue	Dr.	Drive	Mkt.	Market	St.	Street
Bk.	Bank	E.	East	Ms.	Mews	Ter.	Terrace
Bri.	Bridge	Embk.	Embankment	Mt.	Mount	Vills.	Villas
Cen.	Centre,Central	Fm.	Farm	N.	North	Vw.	View
Ch.	Church	Gdns.	Gardens	Par.	Parade	W.	West
Circ.	Circle	Gra.	Grange	Pas.	Passage	Wd.	Wood
Clo.	Close	Grn.	Green	Pk.	Park	Wf.	Wharf
Cor.	Corner	Gro.	Grove	Pl.	Place	Wk.	Walk
Cotts.	Cottages	Ho.	House	Rd.	Road		
Cres.	Crescent	La.	Lane	Ri.	Rise		

Post Town Abbreviations

Hol.	Holywood	New.	Newtownabbey

NOTES

This index contains some street names in standard text which are followed by another street named in italics. In these cases the street in standard text does not actually appear on the map due to insufficient space but can be located close to the street named in italics.

Abbey Ct. BT5	19	Q9
Abbey Gdns.		
Abbey Dale Ct. BT14	9	D5
Abbey Dale Cres. BT14	9	D5
Abbey Dale Dr. BT14	9	D5
Abbey Dale Gdns. BT14	9	D5
Abbey Dale Par. BT14	9	D5
Abbey Dale Pk. BT14	9	D5
Abbey Gdns. BT5	19	P9
Abbey Pk. BT5	19	P9
Abbey Pl., Hol. BT18	7	P3
Abbey Ring		
Abbey Ring, Hol. BT18	7	P3
Abbey Rd. BT5	19	P9
Abbey St. W. BT15	10	H6
Hanna St.		
Abbots Wd., Hol. BT18	7	P3
Abercorn St. BT9	22	G10
Abercorn St. N. BT12	15	F8
Abercorn Wk. BT12	15	F8
Abercorn St. N.		
Aberdeen St. BT13	15	F7
Abetta Par. BT5	17	L9
Abingdon Dr. BT12	15	G9
Abingdon St.		
Abingdon St. BT12	15	G9
Abyssinia St. BT12	15	F8
Abyssinia Wk. BT12	15	F8
Abyssinia St.		
Academy St. BT1	16	H7
Acton St. BT13	15	F7
Adam St. BT15	10	H6
Adela Pl. BT14	16	G7
Adela St. BT14	16	G7
Adelaide Chase BT9	22	F11
Adelaide Par. BT9	22	G11
Adelaide Pk. BT9	22	F11
Adelaide St. BT2	16	H8
Agincourt Av. BT7	22	H10
Agincourt St. BT7	22	H10
Agnes Clo. BT13	15	G7
Agnes St. BT13	15	G7
Agra St. BT7	22	H10
Aigburth Pk. BT4	17	M8
Ailesbury Cres. BT7	22	H11
Ailesbury Dr. BT7	23	J11
Ailesbury Gdns. BT7	23	J12
Ailesbury Rd. BT7	23	J11
Ainsworth Av. BT13	15	E7
Ainsworth Dr. BT13	15	E7
Ainsworth Par. BT13	15	E7
Vara Dr.		
Ainsworth Pas. BT13	15	E7
Ainsworth St. BT13	15	E7
Airport Rd. BT3	17	L7
Airport Rd. W. BT3	12	M5
Aitnamona Cres. BT11	20	C10
Alanbrooke Rd. BT6	24	L11
Albany Pl. BT13	15	F7
Albany Sq. BT13	15	F7
Crimea St.		
Albert Bri. BT1	16	J8
Albert Bri. BT5	16	J8
Albert Rd. BT5	17	K8
Albert Ct. BT12	15	G8
Albert Dr. BT6	23	L11
Albert Pl. BT12	15	G8
Albert St.		
Albert Sq. BT1	16	H7
Albert St. BT12	15	G8
Albert Ter. BT12	16	G8
Albert St.		
Albertville Dr. BT14	10	F6
Albion La. BT7	16	H9
Botanic Av.		
Albion St. BT12	16	G9
Alder Clo. BT5	25	O11
Alexander Ct. BT15	5	H3
Alexander Rd. BT6	24	L10
Alexandra Av. BT15	10	H5
Alexandra Gdns. BT15	10	G4
Alexandra Pk., Hol. BT18	7	Q3
Alexandra Pk. Av. BT15	10	G5
Alexandra Pl., Hol. BT18	7	Q2
Church Vw.		
Alford Pk. BT5	25	Q10
Melfort Dr.		
Alfred St. BT2	16	H8

Alliance Av. BT14	9	E5
Alliance Cres. BT14	9	F5
Alliance Dr. BT14	9	E5
Alliance Gdns. BT14	9	E5
Alliance Par. BT14	9	E5
Alliance Pk. BT14	9	E5
Alliance Rd. BT14	9	E5
Alloa St. BT14	10	G6
Allworthy Av. BT14	10	G6
Altcar St. BT5	17	K8
Altigarron Ct. BT12	14	D9
Westrock Gdns.		
Alton Ct. BT13	16	H7
Alton St. BT13	16	G7
Ambleside St. BT13	15	F7
Amcomri St. BT12	15	E9
Amelia St. BT2	16	H9
Ampere St. BT6	23	K10
Anderson Ct. BT5	16	J8
Anderson St. BT5	16	J8
Andersonstown BT12	15	F8
Falls Rd.		
Andersonstown Cres. BT11	21	D10
Andersonstown Dr. BT11	21	D10
Andersonstown Gdns. BT11	21	D10
Andersonstown Gro. BT11	21	D11
Andersonstown Par. BT11	21	D10
Andersonstown Gdns.		
Andersonstown Pk. BT11	21	D11
Andersonstown Pk. S. BT11	21	D11
Andersonstown Pk. W. BT11	21	D11
Andersonstown Pl. BT11	21	D11
Andersonstown Pk.		
Andersonstown Rd. BT11	20	C12
Anglesea St. BT13	15	F7
Beresford St.		
Ann St. BT1	16	H8
Annadale Av. BT7	23	J12
Annadale Cres. BT7	22	H11
Annadale Dr. BT7	22	H11
Annadale Embk. BT7	22	H11
Annadale Flats BT7	22	H11
Annadale Gdns. BT7	22	H11
Annadale Grn. BT7	22	H11
Annadale Gro. BT7	22	H11
Annadale Ter. BT7	22	H11
Annalee Ct. BT14	10	G6
Avonbeg Clo.		
Annalee St. BT14	10	G6
Annesley St. BT14	16	G7
Annesley St. BT15	4	G3
Antrim Rd.		
Annsboro St. BT13	15	F8
Sugarfield St.		
Antigua Ct. BT14	10	F6
Glenpark St.		
Antigua St. BT14	10	F6
Antrim Rd. BT15	10	G4
Apollo Rd. BT12	21	E10
Appleton Pk. BT11	20	C12
Apsley St. BT7	16	H9
Arbour St. BT14	10	F6
Ard-na-va Rd. BT12	15	E9
Ardavon Pk. BT15	10	H4
Ardcarn Dr. BT5	19	Q9
Ardcarn Grn. BT5	19	Q9
Ardcarn Pk. BT5	19	R9
Ardcarn Way BT5	19	Q9
Ardenlee Av. BT6	23	K10
Ardenlee Dr. BT6	23	K10
Ardenlee Gdns. BT6	23	K10
Ardenlee Par. BT6	23	K10
Ardenlee St. BT6	23	K10
Ardenvohr St. BT6	17	K9
Ardgowan Dr. BT6	17	L9
Ardgowan St. BT6	23	K10
Ardgreenan Cres. BT4	18	N8
Campbell Pk. Av.		
Ardgreenan Dr. BT4	18	N8
Ardgreenan Gdns. BT4	18	N8
Ardgreenan Mt. BT4	18	N8
Wandsworth Par.		
Ardgreenan Pl. BT4	18	N8
Wandsworth Par.		
Ardilaun St. BT4	17	K8
Lackagh Ct.		
Ardila Ct. BT14	10	F6
Ardila Dr.		

Ardilea Dr. BT14	10	F6
Ardilea St. BT14	10	F6
Ardkeen Cres. BT6	24	M11
Ardlee Av., Hol. BT18	7	Q3
Ardmillan BT15	10	G4
Ardmonagh Gdns. BT11	14	C9
Ardmonagh Par. BT11	14	C9
Ardmonagh Way BT11	14	C9
Ardmore Av. BT7	23	J12
Ardmore Av. BT10	20	C13
Ardmore Av., Hol. BT18	7	R3
Ardmore Ct. BT10	20	C13
Ardmore Dr. BT10	20	C13
Ardmore Heights, Hol. BT18	7	R3
Ardmore Pk. BT10	20	C13
Ardmore Pk., Hol. BT18	7	R2
Ardmore Pk. S. BT10	20	C13
Ardmore Rd., Hol. BT18	7	R2
Ardmore Ter., Hol. BT18	7	R2
Ardmoulin Av. BT13	15	G8
Ardmoulin Clo. BT13	15	G8
Ardmoulin Av.		
Ardmoulin Pl. BT12	15	G8
Divis Flats		
Ardmoulin St. BT12	15	G8
Ardmoulin Ter. BT12	15	G8
Divis Flats		
Ardnaclowney Dr. BT12	15	E9
Ardnagreena Gdns., Hol. BT18	13	P4
Ardoyne Av. BT14	9	F6
Ardoyne Ct. BT14	9	F6
Ardoyne Av.		
Ardoyne Pl. BT14	9	F6
Ardoyne Av.		
Ardoyne Rd. BT14	9	E5
Ardoyne Sq. BT14	9	F6
Ardoyne Av.		
Ardoyne Village BT14	9	E5
Ardoyne Rd.		
Ardoyne Wk. BT14	9	F6
Ardoyne Av.		
Ardpatrick Gdns. BT6	24	M10
Ardvarna Cres. BT4	18	N7
Ardvarna Pk. BT4	18	N7
Argyle St. BT13	15	F8
Argyle St. BT13	15	F8
Ariel St. BT13	15	G7
Arizona St. BT11	21	D10
Arlington Pk. BT10	20	B13
Armitage Clo. BT4	17	L7
Harkness Par.		
Arney St. BT6	23	K12
Arnon St. BT13	16	H7
Arosa Par. BT15	11	J5
Arran Ct. BT5	17	K8
Thompson St.		
Arran St. BT5	17	K8
Artana St. BT7	23	J10
Arthur La. BT1	16	H8
Arthur Pl. BT1	16	H8
Arthur St.		
Arthur Sq. BT1	16	H8
Arthur St. BT1	16	H8
Arundel Cts. BT12	15	G9
Arundel Ho. BT12	15	F9
Arundel Cts.		
Arundel Wk. BT12	15	F9
Roden Pas.		
Ascot Gdns. BT5	25	O10
Ascot Ms. BT5	24	N10
Knockmount Pk.		
Ascot Pk. BT5	25	O10
Ash Grn., Hol. BT18	7	P3
Loughview Av.		
Ashbourne Ct. BT4	18	N8
Ashbrook Cres. BT4	18	N7
Ashbrook Dr.		
Ashbrook Dr. BT4	18	N7
Ashburn Grn. BT4	18	N7
Ashmount Pk.		
Ashburne Ms. BT7	16	H9
Salisbury St.		
Ashburne Pl. BT7	16	H9
Salisbury St.		
Ashburne St. BT7	16	H9
Ashburne St. BT7	17	L8
Ashdale St. BT5	17	L8
Ashdene Dr. BT15	10	H5

Name	Page	Grid
Ashfield Ct. BT15	10	H5
Ashfield Cres. BT15	10	H5
Ashfield Dr. BT15	10	H5
Ashfield Gdns. BT15	10	H5
Ashford Grn. BT4	18	N7
Ashmount Pk.		
Ashgrove Pk. BT14	10	F5
Ashleigh Manor BT9	22	G10
Ashley Av. BT9	22	F10
Ashley Dr. BT9	22	F10
Ashley Gdns. BT15	5	H3
Ashley Ms. BT9	22	G10
Ashmore Pl. BT13	15	F8
Ashmore St. BT13	15	F8
Ashmount Gro. BT4	18	N7
Ashmount Pk.		
Ashmount Pk. BT4	18	N7
Ashmount Pl. BT4	18	N7
Ashton Av. BT10	20	C13
Ashton Pk. BT10	20	C13
Ashton St. BT15	10	H6
Aston Gdns. BT4	18	N8
Astoria Gdns. BT15	18	N9
Athol St. BT12	16	G8
Athol St. La. BT12	16	G8
Athol St.		
Atlantic Av. BT15	10	G6
Aughrim Pk. BT12	16	G9
Austin St. BT5	17	K8
Ava Av. BT7	22	H11
Ava Cres. BT7	22	H11
Ava Dr. BT7	22	H11
Ava Gdns. BT7	22	H11
Ava Par. BT7	22	H11
Ava Pk. BT7	22	H11
Ava St. BT7	23	J11
Avoca St. BT14	10	G6
Avonbeg Clo. BT14	10	G6
Avonbeg St. BT14	10	G6
Avondale St. BT5	17	L9
Avoniel Dr. BT5	17	L9
Avoniel Par. BT5	17	L9
Avoniel Rd. BT5	17	L8
Avoniel St. BT6	17	K9
Beersbridge Rd.		
Avonorr Dr. BT5	17	L9
Avonvale BT4	13	O6
Ayr St. BT15	11	J5
Azamor St. BT13	15	F7
Back Mt. St. BT5	17	K9
Bainesmore Dr. BT13	15	E7
Balaclava St. BT12	15	F8
Balfour Av. BT7	23	J10
Balholm Dr. BT14	9	E6
Balkan Ct. BT12	15	F8
Balkan St. BT12	15	F8
Ballagh Beg BT11	20	C11
Bearnagh Dr.		
Ballarat Ct. BT6	16	J9
Ballarat St. BT6	16	J9
Ballycarry St. BT14	10	F6
Ballynure St.		
Ballycastle Ct. BT14	10	F6
Ballycastle St. BT14	10	F6
Ballynure St.		
Ballyclare Ct. BT14	10	F6
Ballyclare St. BT14	10	F6
Ballynure St.		
Ballyclare Way BT14	10	F6
Ballynure St.		
Ballygomartin Dr. BT13	14	D7
Ballygomartin Pk. BT13	15	E7
Ballygomartin Rd. BT13	14	C8
Ballygowan Rd. BT5	24	N11
Ballyhanwood Rd. BT5	25	Q11
Ballymacarrett Rd. BT4	17	K8
Ballymacarrett Walkway BT4	17	L8
Dee St.		
Ballymagarry La. BT13	14	D7
Ballymena Ct. BT14	10	F6
Ballymoney St.		
Ballymenoch Pk., Hol. BT18	7	Q1
Ballymiscaw Rd., Hol. BT18	19	Q7
Ballymoney Ct. BT14	10	F6
Ballymoney St.		
Ballymoney St. BT14	10	F6
Ballymurphy Cres. BT12	14	D9
Ballymurphy Dr. BT12	14	D9
Ballymurphy Par. BT12	14	D9
Ballymurphy Rd. BT12	14	D9
Ballymurphy St. BT12	15	E9
Ballynure St. BT14	10	F6
Ballynure Way BT14	10	F6
Ballynure St.		
Ballysillan Av. BT14	9	E4
Ballysillan Cres. BT14	9	E4
Ballysillan Dr. BT14	9	E4
Ballysillan Pk. BT14	9	E3
Ballysillan Rd. BT14	9	D5
Balmoral Av. BT9	21	E12
Balmoral Ct. BT9	21	E12
Upper Lisburn Rd.		
Balmoral Dr. BT9	21	E12
Balmoral Gdns. BT9	21	E12
Balmoral Link BT12	21	E11
Balmoral Ms. BT9	21	F13
Balmoral Pk. (Finaghy) BT10	21	D13
Balmoral Rd. BT12	21	E11
Baltic Av. BT15	10	G5
Banbury St. BT4	17	L8
Bandon St. BT4	10	G6
Bangor Rd., Hol. BT18	7	Q2
Bank St. BT1	16	H8
Bankmore Sq. BT7	16	H9
Bankmore St.		
Bankmore St. BT7	16	H9
Bann Ct. BT14	10	G6
Shannon St.		
Bannagh Cor. BT6	23	K12
Bantry St. BT13	15	F8
Bapaume Av. BT6	24	L11
Barbour St. BT15	10	H4
Shore Rd.		
Barginnis St. BT14	9	E5
Crumlin Rd.		
Barnetts Cres. BT5	19	P9
Barnetts Grn. BT5	19	P9
Barnetts Rd. BT5	18	O9
Baroda Dr. BT7	23	J10
Baroda Par. BT7	23	J10
Baroda St. BT7	22	H10
Barrack St. BT12	16	G8
Barrington Gdns. BT12	15	G9
Abingdon St.		
Barrington St. BT12	15	G9
Donegall Rd.		
Baskin St. BT5	17	K8
Bath Ter., Hol. BT18	7	Q2
Bathgate Dr. BT4	18	M8
Batley St. BT5	17	L9
Battenberg St. BT13	15	F7
Battons La., Hol. BT18	7	Q2
Church Vw.		
Bawnmore Ct. BT9	21	F12
Bawnmore Rd.		
Bawnmore Rd. BT9	21	F12
Bearnagh Dr. BT11	20	C11
Bearnagh Glen BT11	20	C11
Bearnagh Dr.		
Bedford St. BT2	16	H8
Beech End, Hol. BT18	7	P3
Beech Pk. BT6	24	M11
Beech Wd., Hol. BT18	7	R1
Beeches, The BT7	23	J12
Hampton Pk.		
Beechfield Ct. BT5	17	K8
Beechfield St.		
Beechfield St. BT5	17	K8
Beechgrove Av. BT6	23	K13
Beechgrove Cres. BT6	23	L12
Beechgrove Dr. BT6	23	K12
Beechgrove Gdns. BT6	23	K13
Beechgrove Pk. BT6	23	K12
Beechgrove Ri. BT6	23	K13
Beechlands BT9	22	G11
Beechmount Av. BT12	15	E9
Beechmount Cres. BT12	15	E9
Beechmount Dr. BT12	15	E9
Beechmount Gro. BT12	15	E8
Beechmount Par. BT12	15	E9
Beechmount Pk. BT10	21	D13
Beechmount Pas. BT12	15	E8
Beechmount St. BT12	15	E9
Beechnut Pl. BT14	10	F5
Beechpark St. BT14	10	F5
Oldpark Rd.		
Beechview Pk. BT12	14	D9
Beechwood St. BT5	17	L8
Beersbridge Rd. BT5	17	K9
Beggs St. BT12	16	G9
Beit St. BT12	15	F9
Belair St. BT13	15	E7
Belfast Rd., Hol. BT18	7	P3
Belgrave St. BT13	15	G7
Belgravia Av. BT9	22	G10
Bell Clo. BT13	15	F7
Booth St.		
Bellevue St. BT13	15	F8
Bellfield Ct. BT12	14	C9
Belmont Av. BT4	18	M8
Belmont Av. W. BT4	18	N8
Belmont Ch. Rd. BT4	18	N8
Belmont Clo. BT4	18	N8
Belmont Av.		
Belmont Dr. BT4	18	O8
Belmont Gra. BT4	18	N8
Belmont Ms. BT4	18	M8
Belmont Pk. BT4	18	N8
Belmont Pl. BT4	18	N8
Sydenham Av.		
Belmont Rd. BT4	18	M8
Belmore St. BT7	22	H10
Belvedere Manor BT9	22	G11
Belvedere Pk. BT9	22	H12
Belvoir St. BT5	17	K8
Benares St. BT13	15	F8
Benbradagh Gdns. BT11	20	C11
Benburb St. BT12	21	F10
Bendigo St. BT6	16	J9
Bennett Dr. BT14	10	G5
Brookvale Av.		
Bennetts Pl. BT6	23	J11
Ravenhill Rd.		
Benraw Gdns. BT11	20	C11
Benraw Rd.		
Benraw Grn. BT11	20	C11
Benraw Rd. BT11	20	C11
Benraw Ter. BT11	20	C11
Benraw Rd.		
Bentham Dr. BT12	15	G9
Bentinck St. BT15	10	H6
Benview Av. BT14	9	E4
Benview Par. BT14	9	E4
Benview Pk. BT14	9	E4
Benwee Pk. BT11	20	B12
Beresford St. BT13	15	F7
Berlin St. BT13	15	F7
Berry St. BT1	16	H8
Berwick Rd. BT14	9	E5
Bethany St. BT4	18	N8
Beverley St. BT13	15	G8
Bilston Rd. BT14	9	D4
Bingnian Dr. BT11	20	C11
Bingnian Way BT11	20	C11
Birch Dr., Hol. BT18	7	Q2
Bisley St. BT13	15	F7
Black Mountain Av. BT13	14	D8
Black Mountain Gro. BT13	14	D8
Black Mountain Par. BT13	14	D8
Black Mountain Pas. BT13	14	D8
Black Mountain Pk. BT13	14	D8
Black Mountain Pl. BT13	14	D8
Black Mountain Wk. BT13	14	D7
Black Mountain Way BT13	14	D8
Blacks St. BT11	20	B13
Blacks Rd. BT10	20	A12
Blacks Rd. BT11	20	A12
Blackwater Way BT12	15	F9
Brassey St.		
Blackwood St. BT7	23	J11
Bladon Ct. BT9	22	G13
Bladon Dr. BT9	22	F12
Bladon Pk. BT9	22	G12
Blakeley Ter. BT12	16	G9
Rowland Way		
Blakiston Gdns. BT5	24	M10
Blaney St. BT13	15	F7
Crimea St.		
Bleach Grn. BT14	9	D4
Bleach Grn. Ct. BT12	14	C9
Bleach Grn. Ter. BT12	14	C9
Bleach Grn. Ct.		
Blenheim Dr. BT6	24	L10
Blondin St. BT12	16	G9
Bloomdale St. BT5	17	L8
Bloomfield Av. BT5	17	L8
Bloomfield Ct. BT5	17	L9
Bloomfield Cres. BT5	17	L9
Bloomfield Dr. BT5	17	L9
Bloomfield Gdns. BT5	17	M9
Bloomfield Par. BT5	17	L9
Bloomfield Pk. BT5	17	M9
Bloomfield Pk. W. BT5	17	M9
Bloomfield Rd. BT5	17	M9
Bloomfield St. BT5	17	L9
Blythe St. BT12	16	G9
Bombay St. BT13	15	F8
Bond St. BT7	16	H9
Boodles Hill BT14	8	C4
Mountainhill Rd.		
Boodles La. BT14	9	D4
Bootle St. BT13	15	F7
Botanic Av. BT7	16	H9
Botanic Ct. BT7	22	H10
Agincourt Av.		
Boucher Cres. BT12	21	E11
Boucher Pl. BT12	21	E11
Boucher Rd. BT9	21	E12
Boucher Rd. BT12	21	E12
Boucher Way BT12	21	E10
Boundary St. BT13	15	G8
Boundary Wk. BT13	16	G7
Boundary Way BT13	16	G7
Bowness St. BT13	15	F7
Boyd St. BT13	16	G8
Boyne Bri. BT12	16	G9
Boyne Ct. BT12	16	G9
Rowland Way		
Bracken St. BT13	15	E7
Bradbury Pl. BT7	16	H9
Bradford Pl. BT8	23	J13
Church Rd.		
Bradford Sq. BT13	16	J7
Steam Mill La.		
Bradys St. BT13	15	G7
Boundary St.		
Brae Hill Cres. BT14	9	D4
Brae Hill Link BT14	9	E4
Brae Hill Rd.		
Brae Hill Par. BT14	9	D4
Brae Hill Pk. BT14	9	D4
Brae Hill Way BT14	9	D4
Braemar St. BT12	15	F9
Braeside Gro. BT5	24	N11
Bramcote St. BT5	17	L9
Brandon Par. BT4	17	L8
Brandon Ter. BT4	17	M8
Brandra St. BT4	17	M8
Braniel Cres. BT5	24	N11
Braniel Pk. BT5	24	N11
Braniel Rd. Lwr. BT5	24	N11
Braniel Way BT5	24	N11
Brantwood St. BT15	10	H5
Brassey St. BT12	15	F9
Bray Clo. BT13	9	E6
Bray Ct. BT13	9	E6
Bray Clo.		
Bray St. BT13	9	E6
Bread St. BT12	15	G8
Brenda Pk. BT11	20	C12
Brenda St. BT5	17	L9
Brentwood Pk. BT5	24	N11
Brianville Pk. BT14	4	F3
Briarwood Pk. BT5	25	P10
Bridge End BT5	16	J8
Bridge End Flyover BT4	16	J8
Bridge End Flyover BT5	16	J8
Bridge St. BT1	16	H8
Bridge St. Pl. BT1	16	H8
Bridge St.		
Bright St. BT5	17	L8
Hornby St.		
Brighton St. BT12	15	E9
Bristol Av. BT15	5	H3
Bristow Dr. BT5	25	Q10

Street	Post	Grid
Bristow Pk. BT9	21	E13
Britannic Dr. BT12	16	G9
Rowland Way		
Britannic Pk. BT12	15	G9
Britannic Ter. BT12	16	G9
Rowland Way		
Brittons Ct. BT12	14	D9
Brittons Dr. BT12	14	D9
Brittons La. BT12	14	D8
Brittons La. BT13	14	D8
Brittons Par. BT12	14	D9
Broadway BT12	21	F10
Broadway Ct. BT12	15	F9
Broadway		
Broadway Par. BT12	21	F10
Bromley St. BT13	15	F7
Brompton Pk. BT14	9	E6
Brook Meadow BT5	25	P10
Brook St., Hol. BT18	7	Q2
Brooke Clo. BT11	20	B12
Brooke Ct. BT11	20	B13
Brooke Cres. BT11	20	B13
Brooke Dr. BT11	20	B13
Brooke Manor BT11	20	B13
Brooke Pk. BT10	20	B13
Brookfield Pl. BT14	9	F6
Brookfield St. BT14	9	F6
Herbert St.		
Brookfield Wk. BT14	9	F6
Brookhill Av. BT14	10	G6
Brookland St. BT9	22	F11
Brookmill Way BT14	9	D4
Brookmount Gdns. BT13	15	F7
Lawnbrook Av.		
Brookmount St. BT13	15	F7
Brookvale Av. BT14	10	G5
Brookvale Dr. BT14	10	G5
Brookvale Par. BT14	10	G5
Brookvale St. BT14	10	G5
Brookville Ct. BT14	10	G5
Broom St. BT13	15	E7
Broomhill Clo. BT9	22	G12
Broomhill Ct. BT9	22	G12
Stranmillis Rd.		
Broomhill Manor BT9	22	G12
Stranmillis Rd.		
Broomhill Pk. BT9	22	G12
Broomhill Pk. Cen. BT9	22	G12
Brougham Ct. BT15	10	H6
Brougham St.		
Brougham St. BT15	10	H6
Broughton Gdns. BT6	23	J10
Broughton Pk. BT6	23	J10
Brown Sq. BT13	16	G7
Brown St. BT13	16	G8
Browns Pk., Hol. BT18	7	R1
Browns Row BT1	16	H7
Academy St.		
Bruce St. BT2	16	H9
Brucevale Ct. BT14	10	G6
Brucevale Pk. BT14	10	G6
Brunel St. BT13	15	G7
Agnes St.		
Brunswick St. BT2	16	H8
Bruslee Way BT15	10	H6
Brussels St. BT13	15	F7
Bryansford Pl. BT6	17	K9
Bryson Ct. BT5	17	K8
Mountforde Rd.		
Bryson Gdns. BT5	17	K8
Mountforde Rd.		
Bryson St. BT5	17	K8
Burmah St. BT7	23	J10
Burnaby Ct. BT12	15	G9
Distillery St.		
Burnaby Pk. BT12	15	G9
Distillery Ct.		
Burnaby Pl. BT12	15	G9
Burnaby Way BT12	15	G9
Burnaby Pl.		
Burntollet Way BT6	23	L11
Burren Way BT6	23	K11
Bute St. BT15	11	J5
Butler St. BT14	9	E6
Butler St. BT14	9	E6
Butler Wk. BT14	9	E6
Byron Pl., Hol. BT18	7	P2
Byron St., Hol. BT18	7	P2
Cabin Hill Gdns. BT5	18	O9
Cabin Hill Ms. BT5	19	P9
Cabin Hill Pk. BT5	18	O9
Cable Clo. BT4	17	K8
Newtownards Rd.		
Cadogan Pk. BT9	22	F11
Cadogan St. BT7	22	H10
Cairnburn Av. BT4	18	O7
Cairnburn Cres. BT4	18	O7
Cairnburn Dell BT4	18	O7
Cairnburn Cres.		
Cairnburn Dr. BT4	18	O7
Cairnburn Gdns. BT4	18	O7
Cairnburn Pk. BT4	18	O7
Cairnburn Rd. BT4	18	O7
Cairns, The BT4	18	N8
Cairns St. BT12	15	F8
Cairo St. BT7	22	H10
Caledon Ct. BT13	15	F7
Caledon St. BT13	15	E7
California Clo. BT13	16	G7
North Boundary St.		
Callan St. BT6	23	K11
Callender St. BT1	16	H8
Calvin St. BT5	17	K9
Camberwell Ter. BT15	10	G5
Cambrai St. BT13	15	F7
Cambridge St. BT15	10	H6
Canning St.		
Camden St. BT9	22	G10
Cameron St. BT7	16	H9
Cameronian Dr. BT5	24	M10
Camlough Pl. BT6	24	M11
Campbell Ct. BT4	18	N8
Campbell Pk. Av. BT4	18	N8
Canada St. BT6	16	J9
McMullans La.		
Candahar St. BT7	22	H11
Canmore Ct. BT13	15	F8
Canmore St.		
Canmore St. BT13	15	F8
Canning Pl. BT15	10	H6
Canning St.		
Canning St. BT15	10	H6
Cannings Ct. BT13	15	G7
Shankill Rd.		
Canterbury St. BT7	22	H10
Canton Ct. BT6	17	K9
Willowfield St.		
Cape St. BT12	15	F8
Cappagh Gdns. BT6	23	K11
South Bk.		
Cappy St. BT6	17	K9
Capstone St. BT9	21	F11
Cardigan Dr. BT14	10	F5
Carew St. BT4	17	L8
Cargill St. BT13	16	G7
Carlingford St. BT6	17	K9
Carlisle Circ. BT14	16	G7
Carlisle Par. BT15	10	H6
Carlisle Rd. BT15	16	H7
Carlisle Sq. BT15	16	H7
Carlisle Ter.		
Carlisle St. BT13	16	G7
Carlisle Ter. BT15	16	H7
Carlisle Wk. BT15	16	H7
Carlisle Ter.		
Carlow St. BT13	15	G8
Carmel St. BT7	22	H10
Carn End, Hol. BT18	7	P3
Carnalea Pl. BT15	10	H6
Carnamena Av. BT6	24	M11
Carnamena Gdns. BT6	24	M11
Carnamena Pk. BT6	24	M11
Carnan St. BT13	15	F7
Carnanmore Gdns. BT11	20	B13
Brooke Dr.		
Carnanmore Pk. BT11	20	A13
Carncaver Rd. BT6	24	M11
Carncoole Pk. BT14	4	F3
Carney Cres. BT6	24	M11
Carnforth St. BT5	17	L8
Carnmore Pl. BT12	14	C9
Whiterock Rd.		
Carnmamona St. BT11	20	C10
Carolan Rd. BT7	23	J12
Carolhill Dr. BT4	18	N7
Carolhill Gdns. BT4	18	N7
Carolhill Pk. BT4	18	N7
Carolina St. BT13	15	F7
Carrick Hill BT1	16	H7
Carrington St. BT6	16	J9
Carr's Glen Pk. BT14	9	E4
Ballysillan Pk.		
Casaeldona Cres. BT6	24	N11
Casaeldona Dr. BT6	24	N11
Casaeldona Ri.		
Casaeldona Gdns. BT6	24	M11
Casaeldona Pk. BT6	24	M11
Casaeldona Ri. BT6	24	M11
Castle Arc. BT1	16	H8
Castle La.		
Castle Av. BT15	5	H3
Castle Chambers BT1	16	H8
Rosemary St.		
Castle Ct. BT6	24	N11
Castle Dr. BT15	5	H3
Castle Gdns. BT15	5	H3
Castle La. BT1	16	H8
Castle Ms. BT6	24	N11
Castle Pk. BT15	4	G3
Castle Pl. BT1	16	H8
Castle St. BT1	16	H8
Castlehill Dr. BT4	19	P8
Castlehill Manor BT4	19	P8
Castlehill Pk. BT4	19	P8
Castlehill Pk. W. BT4	19	P8
Castlehill Rd. BT4	19	P8
Castlekaria Manor BT4	19	P8
Castlemore Av. BT6	24	M11
Castlemore Pk. BT6	24	M11
Castleorr Manor BT4	19	P8
Castlereagh Par. BT5	17	L9
Castlereagh Pl. BT5	17	K9
Castlereagh Rd. BT5	17	L9
Castlereagh St. BT5	17	K9
Castleton Av. BT15	10	H5
York Rd.		
Castleton Gdns. BT15	10	G5
Castleview Ct. BT5	24	N11
Castleview Rd. BT5	19	P9
Castleview Ter. BT4	18	N8
Catherine Pl. BT15	10	H4
Shore Rd.		
Catherine St. BT2	16	H9
Catherine St. N. BT2	16	H8
Cavanmore Gdns. BT11	20	B11
Cavehill Dr. BT15	4	G3
Cavehill Rd. BT15	4	G3
Cavendish Ct. BT12	15	E8
Cavendish Sq. BT12	15	F8
Cavendish St. BT12	15	F8
Cawnpore St. BT13	15	F8
Cedar Av. BT15	10	G5
Cedar Gro., Hol. BT18	13	O5
Centurion St. BT13	15	F7
Centurion Way BT13	15	F7
Lawnbrook Av.		
Century St. BT13	10	F6
Ceylon St. BT13	15	E7
Chadolly St. BT4	17	K8
Chadwick St. BT9	22	F11
Chamberlain St. BT5	17	L8
Chambers St. BT7	16	H9
Channing St. BT5	17	L9
Chapel La. BT1	16	H8
Charlemont St. BT1	16	H8
Garfield St.		
Charles St. S. BT12	16	G9
Charleville Av. BT9	21	F11
Charleville St. BT13	15	F7
Charlotte St. BT7	16	H9
Charnwood Av. BT15	10	G4
Charnwood Ct. BT15	10	G4
Charters Av. BT5	25	P10
Chater St. BT4	17	L8
Tamar St.		
Chatham St. BT14	9	E6
Chatsworth St. BT5	17	K9
Chelsea St. BT4	17	L8
Cheltenham Gdns. BT6	23	K12
Cheltenham Par. BT6	23	K12
Chemical St. BT5	17	K8
Cherryhill BT9	22	G11
Cherrytree BT5	25	P10
Cherrytree Wk. BT5	18	O9
Cherryvalley		
Cherryvalley BT5	18	O9
Cherryvalley Gdns. BT5	25	O10
Cherryvalley Grn. BT5	18	O9
Cherryvalley Pk. BT5	18	O9
Cherryvalley Pk. W. BT5	25	O10
Cherryville St. BT6	17	K9
Chesham Cres. BT6	23	K10
Chesham Dr. BT6	23	K10
Chesham Gdns. BT6	23	K10
Ardenlee Gdns.		
Chesham Gro. BT6	23	K10
Chesham Par. BT6	23	K10
Chesham Pk. BT6	23	K10
Chesham Ter. BT6	23	K10
Ardenlee Gdns.		
Chesterfield Pk. BT6	23	J12
Chestnut Gdns. BT14	10	G5
Cheviot Av. BT4	17	M8
Cheviot St. BT4	17	M8
Chichester Av. BT15	10	G4
Chichester Clo. BT15	10	G4
Chichester Ct. BT15	10	G4
Chichester Gdns. BT15	10	G4
Antrim Rd.		
Chichester Ms. BT15	10	G4
Chichester Pk. Cen.		
Chichester Pk. Cen. BT15	10	G4
Chichester Pk. N. BT15	10	G4
Chichester Pk. S. BT15	10	G4
Chichester Pk. S. BT15	4	G3
Chichester Rd. BT15	4	G3
Chichester St. BT1	16	H8
Chief St. BT13	9	E6
Chlorine Gdns. BT9	22	G11
Chobham St. BT5	17	L8
Christian Pl. BT12	15	G8
Church Av., Hol. BT18	7	Q2
Church Grn., Hol. BT18	7	Q2
Spencer St.		
Church Hill, Hol. BT18	7	Q2
Church La. BT1	16	H8
Church Path BT12	16	G8
Cullingtree Rd.		
Church Rd. BT6	24	M12
Church Rd. BT8	23	J13
Church Rd., Hol. BT18	7	Q2
Church Row BT12	16	G8
Cullingtree Rd.		
Church St. BT1	16	H7
Church Vw., Hol. BT18	7	Q2
Church Vw. Ms., Hol. BT18	7	Q2
Church Wk. BT12	16	G8
Cullingtree Rd.		
Church Wynd BT5	25	Q10
Churchill St. BT15	10	H6
Churchland Clo., Hol. BT18	13	O5
Churchview Ct. BT14	10	F6
Glenview St.		
Cicero Gdns. BT6	24	L10
Circular Rd. BT4	12	N6
City Wk. BT12	16	G9
City Way BT12	16	G9
Clanchattan St. BT15	10	H5
Clandeboye Dr. BT5	17	K8
Clandeboye Gdns. BT5	17	K9
Clandeboye St. BT5	17	K9
Clanmorris St. BT15	10	H6
Clanroy Par. BT4	18	M8
Clara Av. BT5	17	L9
Clara Cres. Lwr. BT5	17	L9
Clara Cres. Upper BT5	17	L9
Clara Pk. BT5	18	N9
Clara Rd. BT5	18	N9
Clara St. BT5	17	L9
Clara Way BT5	18	N9
Clara Way		
Clarawood Cres. BT5	18	N9
Clarawood Dr. BT5	24	N10
Clarawood Gro. BT5	24	N10
Clarawood Pk. BT5	18	N9
Clarawood Wk. BT5	18	N9
Clare Gdns. BT14	9	E3
Clare Glen BT14	9	E4
Clare Hill BT14	9	E3
Clarehill La., Hol. BT18	13	P4

Street	Page	Grid
Deramore Pk. BT9	22	F13
Deramore Pk. S. BT9	22	F13
Deramore St. BT7	23	J11
Derby Ct. BT12	15	G8
Divis St.		
Derby Ter. BT12	15	G8
Divis St.		
Derlett St. BT7	23	J11
Dermott Hill Dr. BT12	14	C9
Dermott Hill Gdns. BT12	14	C8
Dermott Hill Grn. BT12	14	C9
Dermott Hill Gro. BT12	14	C9
Dermott Hill Par. BT12	14	C8
Dermott Hill Pk. BT12	14	C9
Dermott Hill Rd. BT12	14	C8
Dermott Hill Way BT12	14	C8
Derrin Pas. BT11	20	C11
Derry St. BT13	15	F7
Derryvolgie Av. BT9	22	F11
Derwent St. BT4	17	K8
Devenish Ct. BT13	15	F8
Cupar St.		
Devon Par. BT4	17	M7
Devon Par. BT4	17	M7
Devonshire Clo. BT12	15	G8
Devonshire St.		
Devonshire Pl. BT12	15	G8
Devonshire St.		
Devonshire St. BT12	15	G8
Devonshire Way BT12	15	G8
Devonshire St.		
Dewey St. BT13	15	F7
Dhu-Varren Cres. BT13	15	E7
Dhu-Varren Par. BT13	15	E7
Dhu-Varren Pk. BT13	15	E7
Diamond Av. BT10	20	C13
Diamond Gdns. BT10	20	C13
Diamond St. BT13	15	G7
Dover Pl.		
Dill Rd. BT6	24	L11
Disraeli Ct. BT13	15	E7
Disraeli St.		
Disraeli St. BT13	15	E7
Disraeli Wk. BT13	15	E7
Disraeli St.		
Distillery Ct. BT12	15	G9
Distillery St. BT12	15	G9
Distillery Way BT12	15	G9
Distillery St.		
Divis Dr. BT11	21	D10
Divis Flats BT12	15	G8
Divis St. BT12	15	G8
Divismore Cres. BT12	14	C9
Divismore Pk. BT12	14	D8
Divismore Way BT12	14	D8
Dock St. BT15	16	J7
Dock St.		
Dock St. BT15	10	H6
Dock St. Ms. BT15	11	J6
Dock St.		
Donaldson Cres. BT13	9	E6
Donard St. BT6	17	K9
Donegall Av. BT12	22	F10
Donegall Gdns. BT12	22	F10
Donegall La. BT1	16	H7
Donegall Par. BT12	22	F10
Donegall Pk. BT10	21	D13
Donegall Pk. Av. BT15	5	H2
Donegall Pas. BT7	16	H9
Donegall Pl. BT1	16	H8
Donegall Quay BT1	16	J8
Donegall Rd. BT12	15	E9
Donegall Sq. E. BT1	16	H8
Donegall Sq. Ms. BT2	16	H8
Donegall Sq. N. BT1	16	H8
Donegall Sq. S. BT1	16	H8
Donegall Sq. W. BT1	16	H8
Donegall St. BT1	16	H7
Donegall St. Pl. BT1	16	H8
Donegall St.		
Donegore Gdns. BT11	20	A13
Donnybrook St. BT9	22	F10
Donore Ct. BT1	16	H8
King St.		
Donore Pl. BT15	10	H6
Stratheden St.		
Donovan Par. BT6	24	L10
Doon Cotts. BT11	20	A12
Doon Rd. BT11	20	B12
Dorchester St. BT12	15	G9
Donegall Rd.		
Douglas Ct. BT4	18	M8
Dundela Av.		
Dover Ct. BT13	15	G7
Dover St.		
Dover Pl. BT13	15	G7
Dover St. BT13	15	G8
Dover Wk. BT13	15	G7
Dover St.		
Downfine Gdns. BT11	20	C10
Downfine Pk. BT11	20	C10
Downfine Wk. BT11	20	C10
Downfine Pk.		
Downing St. BT13	15	G7
Downpatrick St. BT4	17	L8
Downshire Par. BT5	23	L11
Hamel Dr.		
Downshire Pk. Cen. BT6	24	L12
Downshire Pk. E. BT6	23	L11
Downshire Pk. N. BT6	24	L12
Downshire Pk. S. BT6	24	L12
Downshire Pl. BT2	16	H9
Little Victoria St.		
Downshire Pl., Hol. BT18	7	Q2
Downshire Rd. BT6	23	L12
Downshire Rd., Hol. BT18	7	Q2
Downview Av. BT15	4	G2
Downview Cres. BT15	5	H2
Downview Dr. BT15	5	H2
Downview Gdns. BT15	5	H2
Downview Lo. BT15	5	H2
Downview Ms. BT15	5	H2
Downview Pk. BT15	4	G2
Downview Pk. W. BT15	4	G3
Drenia BT11	20	B13
Drive, The BT9	22	G12
Dromara St. BT7	23	J10
Dromore St. BT6	23	K10
Drumkeen Ct. BT8	23	K13
Drumkeen Manor BT8	23	J13
Saintfield Rd.		
Drumragh End BT6	23	K11
Dublin Rd. BT2	16	H9
Dublin St. BT6	17	K9
Dudley St. BT7	22	H10
Dufferin Rd. BT3	11	J6
Duffield Pk. BT13	14	D7
Duke St. BT5	17	K8
Susan St.		
Dunbar St. BT1	16	H7
Dunblane Av. BT14	9	F5
Dunboyne Pk. BT13	14	D8
Duncairn Av. BT14	10	G6
Duncairn Gdns. BT15	10	G6
Duncairn Par. BT15	10	H6
Duncoole Pk. BT14	4	F3
Duncrue Cres. BT3	11	J4
Duncrue Link BT3	11	J4
Duncrue Pas. BT3	11	J5
Duncrue Pl. BT3	11	J5
Duncrue Rd. BT3	11	J4
Duncrue St. BT3	11	J5
Dundee St. BT13	15	G7
Dundela Av. BT4	18	M8
Dundela Ct. BT4	18	M8
Dundela Cres.		
Dundela Cres. BT4	18	M8
Dundela Dr. BT4	18	M8
Dundela Flats BT4	18	M8
Dundela Gdns. BT4	18	M8
Dundela Pk. BT4	17	M8
Dundela St. BT4	18	M8
Dundela Vw. BT4	18	M8
Dundela Av.		
Duneden Pk. BT14	9	E6
Dunglow Cres. BT11	20	A11
Dunkeld Gdns. BT14	9	F5
Dunlambert Av. BT15	10	H4
Dunlambert Dr. BT15	10	H4
Dunlambert Gdns. BT15	10	H4
Dunlambert Pk. BT15	10	H4
Dunlewey St. BT13	15	F8
Dunlewey Wk. BT13	15	F8
Dunlewey St.		
Dunlops Pl. BT2	16	H9
Cromac St.		
Dunluce Av. BT9	22	F10
Dunmisk Pk. BT11	21	D11
Dunmisk Ter. BT11	21	D11
Commedagh Dr.		
Dunmore Cres. BT15	10	G5
Dunmore Dr. BT15	10	G5
Dunmore St. BT13	15	F8
Dunmoyle St. BT13	15	F7
Dunowen Gdns. BT14	9	F5
Dunraven Av. BT5	17	M9
Dunraven Ct. BT5	17	M9
Dunraven Cres. BT5	17	M9
Dunraven Dr. BT5	17	M9
Dunraven Gdns. BT5	17	M9
Dunraven Par. BT5	17	M9
Dunraven Pk. BT5	17	M9
Dunraven St. BT13	15	G7
Rumford St.		
Dunvegan St. BT6	16	J9
Dunville St. BT12	15	F8
Durham Ct. BT12	16	G8
Durham St.		
Durham Pl. BT12	16	G8
Durham St.		
Durham St. BT12	16	G8
Dysart St. BT12	15	G8
Divis Flats		
Ean Hill, Hol. BT18	7	P2
Earl Clo. BT15	16	H7
Earl Haig Cres. BT6	23	K10
Earl Haig Pk.		
Earl Haig Gdns. BT6	23	K10
Earl Haig Pk. BT6	23	K10
Earl St. BT15	10	H6
Earls Ct., The BT4	18	N8
Bethany Av.		
Earlscourt St. BT12	15	F8
Earlswood Ct. BT4	18	N8
Kincora Av.		
Earlswood Gro. BT4	18	N8
Earlswood Pk. BT4	18	N8
Earlswood Rd. BT4	18	N8
East Bread St. BT5	17	L8
East Bri. St. BT1	16	J8
East Twin Rd. BT3	11	K5
Eastleigh Cres. BT5	18	N9
Eastleigh Dale BT4	18	N8
Eastleigh Dr. BT4	18	N8
Easton Av. BT14	10	G5
Easton Cres. BT14	10	G5
Eblana St. BT7	22	H10
Ebor Dr. BT12	21	F10
Ebor Par. BT12	21	F10
Ebor St. BT12	21	F10
Ebrington Gdns. BT4	18	M8
Eccles St. BT13	15	F7
Economy Pl. BT15	16	H7
Henry St.		
Eden Ct. BT4	18	N8
Edenderry St. BT13	9	F6
Edenmore Dr. BT11	20	B11
Edenvale Cres. BT4	18	M8
Edenvale Dr. BT4	18	M8
Edenvale Gdns. BT4	18	M8
Edenvale Gro. BT4	18	N8
Edenvale Pk. BT4	18	M8
Edgar St. BT5	17	K8
Edgecumbe Dr. BT4	18	N7
Edgecumbe Gdns. BT4	18	N7
Edgecumbe Pk. BT4	18	N7
Edgecumbe Vw. BT4	18	N7
Edgewater Rd. BT3	11	L4
Edinburgh Av., Hol. BT18	7	Q3
Edinburgh St. BT9	22	F10
Edith St. BT5	17	K8
Edlingham St. BT15	10	H6
Edward St. BT1	16	H7
Edwina St. BT13	15	F7
Riga St.		
Egeria St. BT12	15	G9
Eglantine Av. BT9	22	G10
Eglantine Gdns. BT9	22	G10
Eglantine Pl. BT9	22	G10
Eglinton St. BT13	16	G7
Egmont Gdns. BT12	15	G9
Bentham Dr.		
Eia St. BT14	10	G6
Eileen Gdns. BT9	22	F11
Elaine St. BT9	22	H10
Elesington Ct. BT6	23	L11
Mayfair Av.		
Elgin St. BT7	22	H10
Elimgrove St. BT14	10	F5
Eliza Ct. BT7	16	H9
Eliza St.		
Eliza Pl. BT7	16	H9
Eliza St.		
Eliza St. BT7	16	H9
Eliza St. Clo. BT7	16	J9
Eliza St. Ter. BT7	16	H9
Eliza St.		
Elizabeth Rd., Hol. BT18	7	R2
Elm Ct. BT7	16	H9
Elm St. BT7	16	H9
Elmdale St. BT5	17	L9
Elmfield St. BT14	9	E6
Elmwood Av. BT9	22	G10
Elmwood Ms. BT9	22	G10
Elsmere Heights BT5	25	Q10
Elsmere Pk. BT5	25	Q10
Elswick St. BT12	15	E8
Emerald St. BT6	17	K9
Emerson St. BT13	15	F7
Emersons Row BT14	8	C3
Ligoniel Rd.		
Emersons St. BT14	8	C3
Ligoniel Rd.		
Emily Pl. BT15	16	H7
Great Georges St.		
Empire Dr. BT12	15	F9
Empire Par. BT12	15	F9
Empire St. BT12	15	F9
Enfield Dr. BT13	15	E7
Enfield Par. BT13	9	E6
Enfield St. BT13	15	E7
Enid Dr. BT5	18	N9
Enid Par. BT5	18	N9
Epworth St. BT5	17	K9
Erin Way BT7	16	H9
Errigal Pk. BT11	20	C11
Erris Gro. BT11	20	B13
Oranmore Dr.		
Erskine St. BT5	17	K8
Eskdale Gdns. BT14	9	E5
Esmond St. BT13	15	F7
Espie Way BT6	24	M11
Esplanade, The, Hol. BT18	7	P2
Essex St. BT7	22	H10
Esther St. BT15	10	H5
Estoril Ct. BT14	9	E6
Estoril Pk. BT14	9	E6
Ethel St. BT9	22	F11
Etna Dr. BT14	9	F5
Eureka Dr. BT12	16	G9
Euston Par. BT6	17	L9
Euston St. BT6	17	K9
Euterpe St. BT12	15	G9
Evelyn Av. BT5	17	M8
Evelyn Gdns. BT15	10	G4
Eversleigh St. BT6	17	K9
Cherryville St.		
Everton Dr. BT5	23	L12
Evewilliam Pk. BT15	10	G4
Evolina St. BT15	10	H6
Ewarts Pl. BT14	10	F6
Exchange Pl. BT1	16	H8
Donegall St.		
Exchange St. BT1	16	H7
Exchange St. W. BT1	16	H7
Excise Wk. BT12	15	G9
Faburn Pk. BT14	9	D5
Factory St. BT5	17	L8
East Bread St.		
Fairfax Ct. BT14	10	F6
Fairhill Gdns. BT15	5	H3
Fairhill Pk. BT15	5	H3
Fairhill Wk. BT15	5	H3

Street	Page	Grid
Fairhill Way BT15	5	H3
Fairview St. BT13	15	G7
Hopewell Av.		
Fairway Gdns. BT5	25	O11
Falcarragh Dr. BT11	20	A12
Falcon Rd. BT12	21	F11
Falcon Way BT12	21	F11
Falcon Rd.		
Falls Ct. BT13	15	F8
Conway Link		
Falls Rd. BT11	21	D10
Falls Rd. BT12	21	D10
Fallswater Dr. BT12	15	F8
Falls Rd.		
Fallswater St. BT12	15	E9
Fane St. BT9	22	F10
Farmhurst Grn. BT5	25	P10
Farmhurst Way BT5	25	P10
Farnham St. BT7	23	J10
Farringdon Ct. BT14	9	E5
Farringdon Gdns. BT14	9	E5
Fashoda St. BT5	17	L9
Federation St. BT6	23	K10
Felt St. BT12	16	G9
Ferguson Dr. BT4	18	M8
Fern St. BT4	17	L8
Frome St.		
Ferndale Ct. BT9	21	F11
Lisburn Rd.		
Ferndale St. BT9	21	F11
Fernvale St. BT4	17	M7
Fernwood St. BT7	23	J11
Fife St. BT15	10	H5
Fifth St. BT13	15	F7
Finaghy Rd. N. BT10	20	C13
Finaghy Rd. N. BT10	20	C12
Finaghy Rd. N. BT11	20	C12
Finchley Dr. BT4	13	O6
Finchley Gdns. BT4	13	O6
Finchley Pk.		
Finchley Pk. BT4	13	O6
Finchley Vale BT4	13	O6
Fingal St. BT13	9	E6
Fingals Ct. BT13	15	G8
Finmore Ct. BT4	17	K8
Newtownards Rd.		
Finn Sq. BT13	15	G8
Finsbury St. BT6	23	K10
Finvoy St. BT5	17	M8
Firmount BT15	10	G4
Firmount Ct., Hol. BT18	13	P4
Firmount Cres., Hol. BT18	13	P4
First St. BT13	15	F8
Fisherwick Pl. BT1	16	H8
College Sq. E.		
Fitzroy Av. BT7	22	H10
Fitzwilliam Av. BT7	23	J11
Fitzwilliam St. BT9	22	G10
Flax St. BT14	9	F6
Flaxton Pl. BT14	9	D4
Old Mill Rd.		
Fleetwood St. BT14	16	G7
Crumlin Rd.		
Flora St. BT5	17	L9
Florence Ct. BT13	15	G7
Florence Pl. BT13	15	G7
Florence Sq. BT13	15	G7
Florence Wk. BT13	15	G7
Hopewell Av.		
Florenceville Av. BT7	23	J11
Florenceville Dr. BT7	23	J11
Florida Dr. BT6	17	K9
Florida St. BT6	17	K9
Flush Dr. BT6	23	K10
Flush Gdns. BT6	23	K11
Flush Grn. BT6	23	K11
Flush Pk. BT6	23	K12
Fodnamona Ct. BT11	20	C10
Aitnamona Cres.		
Forest Hill BT9	22	F13
Forest St. BT12	15	E8
Forfar St. BT12	15	E8
Formby Pk. BT14	9	E4
Forster St. BT13	15	G7
Ariel St.		
Forsythe St. BT13	15	G7
Dover Pl.		
Fort St. BT12	15	E8
Forth Par. BT13	15	E7
Forthbrook St. BT13	14	C8
Ballygomartin Rd.		
Forthriver Clo. BT13	9	D5
Forthriver Cotts. BT14	9	E5
Ballysillan Rd.		
Forthriver Cres. BT13	9	D5
Forthriver Dale BT13	9	D5
Forthriver Dr. BT13	9	D5
Forthriver Grn. BT13	9	D5
Forthriver Link BT13	9	D5
Forthriver Par. BT13	8	C5
Forthriver Pk. BT13	8	C5
Forthriver Pas. BT13	9	D6
Forthriver Rd. BT13	9	D5
Forthriver Way BT13	9	D6
Fortuna St. BT12	15	G9
Fortwilliam Ct. BT15	10	G4
Fortwilliam Pk.		
Fortwilliam Cres. BT15	10	H4
Fortwilliam Dr. BT15	4	G3
Fortwilliam Gdns. BT15	10	G4
Fortwilliam Gra. BT15	10	H4
Fortwilliam Par. BT15	10	H4
Fortwilliam Pk. BT15	10	G4
Fountain La. BT1	16	H8
Fountain Ms. BT1	16	H8
Fountain St.		
Fountain St. BT1	16	H8
Fountain St. N. BT15	10	H6
New Lo. Rd.		
Fountainville Av. BT9	22	G10
Fox Row BT13	16	G8
Foxglove St. BT5	17	L9
Foyle Ct. BT14	10	G6
Francis St. BT1	16	H8
Frank Pl. BT5	17	K9
Castlereagh St.		
Frank St. BT5	17	K9
Franklin St. BT2	16	H8
Franklin St. Pl. BT2	16	H8
Franklin St.		
Fraser Pas. BT4	17	K8
Wolff Clo.		
Frederick La. BT1	16	H7
Frederick St.		
Frederick Pl. BT1	16	H7
Frederick St.		
Frederick St. BT1	16	H7
Frenchpark St. BT12	21	F10
Friendly Pl. BT7	16	J9
Friendly St.		
Friendly Row BT7	16	J9
Friendly St. BT7	16	J8
Friendly Way BT7	16	J8
Friendly St.		
Frome St. BT4	17	L8
Fruithill Pk. BT11	20	C10
Fulton St. BT7	16	H9
Gaffikin St. BT12	16	G9
Gainsborough Dr. BT15	10	H5
Galwally Av. BT8	23	J13
Galwally Pk. BT8	23	J12
Galway Pk. (Dundonald) BT16	19	R9
Galway St. BT12	16	G8
Gamble St. BT1	16	H7
Gardiner Pl. BT13	16	G7
Gardiner St. BT13	16	G8
Garfield St. BT1	16	H8
Garmoyle St. BT15	16	J7
Garnerville Dr. BT4	13	O6
Garnerville Gdns. BT4	13	O6
Garnerville Gro. BT4	13	O6
Garnerville Pk. BT4	13	O6
Garnerville Rd. BT4	13	O6
Garnet St. BT12	15	F8
Garnock BT11	20	B13
Garranard Manor BT4	18	N7
Garranard Pk. BT4	18	N7
Gartree Pl. BT11	20	B11
Garvey Glen BT11	20	A12
Suffolk Rd.		
Gawn St. BT4	17	L8
Geary Rd. BT5	25	P10
Geneva Gdns. BT9	22	H12
Genoa St. BT12	15	G9
Geoffrey St. BT13	15	F7
Georges La. E. BT6	23	J11
Ravenhill Rd.		
Ghent Pl. BT13	15	F7
Sydney St. W.		
Ghent St. BT13	15	F7
Gibson Pk. Av. BT6	23	L10
Gibson Pk. Dr. BT6	23	L10
Cregagh Rd.		
Gibson Pk. Gdns. BT6	23	L10
Gibson St. BT12	15	F8
Gilbourne Ct. BT5	25	P10
Gilnahirk Av. BT5	25	P10
Gilnahirk Cres. BT5	25	P10
Gilnahirk Dr. BT5	25	P10
Gilnahirk Pk. BT5	25	P10
Gilnahirk Ri. BT5	25	P10
Gilnahirk Rd. BT5	19	P9
Gilnahirk Rd. W. BT5	25	O11
Gilnahirk Wk. BT5	25	P10
Gipsy St. BT7	23	J11
Glandore Av. BT15	10	G5
Glandore Dr. BT15	10	G4
Glandore Gdns. BT15	10	G4
Glandore Par. BT15	10	H5
Ashfield Gdns.		
Glanleam Dr. BT15	10	G5
Glantane St. BT15	10	G4
Glantrasna Dr. BT15	10	H4
Glanworth Dr. BT15	10	G4
Glanworth Gdns. BT15	10	G5
Glasgow St. BT15	11	J5
Glassmullin Gdns. BT11	20	B11
Glastonbury Av. BT15	4	G3
Glen, The BT15	10	G5
Glen Brae, Hol. BT18	7	R3
Glen Cres. BT11	21	D10
Glen Ebor Heights BT4	13	O6
Glenmachan Rd.		
Glen Ebor St. BT4	13	O6
Glen Par. BT11	21	D10
Glen Ri. BT5	24	N10
Glen Rd. BT4	19	P7
Glen Rd. BT5	24	N11
Glen Rd. BT11	20	A11
Glen Rd. BT12	15	F8
Falls Rd.		
Glenalina Cres. BT12	14	D9
Glenalina Gdns. BT12	14	D9
Glenalina Cres.		
Glenalina Grn. BT12	14	D9
Glenalina Cres.		
Glenalina Pk. BT12	14	D9
Glenalina Pas. BT12	14	D9
Glenalina Rd.		
Glenalina Rd. BT12	14	D9
Glenallen St. BT5	17	K8
Glenalpin St. BT12	16	H9
Glenard Brook BT14	10	G5
Glenbank Dr. BT14	9	D5
Glenbank Par. BT14	9	D5
Leroy St.		
Glenbank Pl. BT14	9	D5
Glenbrook Av. BT5	17	M9
Glenbryn Dr. BT14	9	E5
Glenbryn Gdns. BT14	9	E5
Glenbryn Par. BT14	9	E5
Glenbryn Pk. BT14	9	E5
Glenburn All. BT12	16	G9
Charles St. S.		
Glenburn Pk. BT14	10	G4
Glencairn Cres. BT13	9	E6
Glencairn Pas. BT13	9	D5
Glencairn Rd. BT13	8	C5
Glencairn St. BT13	9	E6
Glencairn Wk. BT13	9	D5
Glencairn Way BT13	9	D6
Glencolin Av. BT11	20	A11
Glencolin Ct. BT11	20	A11
Glencolin Dr. BT11	20	A11
Glencolin Gro. BT11	20	A11
Glencolin Heights BT11	20	A11
Glencolin Pk. BT11	20	A11
Glencolin Ri. BT11	20	A11
Glencolin Wk. BT11	20	A11
Glencolin Way BT11	20	A11
Glencollyer St. BT15	10	H5
Glencourt BT11	21	D10
Glencregagh Ct. BT6	23	K13
Glencregagh Dr. BT6	23	K13
Glencregagh Pk. BT6	23	K13
Glencregagh Rd. BT8	23	K13
Glendarragh Ms. BT4	13	O5
Glendhu Gro. BT4	13	O5
Glendhu Manor BT4	13	O6
Glendhu Pk. BT4	13	O6
Glendower St. BT6	23	K10
Glenfarne St. BT13	15	F7
Agnes St.		
Glengall La. BT12	16	H8
Glengall St.		
Glengall Ms. BT12	16	G8
Glengall St.		
Glengall St. BT12	16	G8
Glengoland Cres. (Dunmurry) BT17	20	A12
Glengoland Gdns. (Dunmurry) BT17	20	A12
Glengoland Par. (Dunmurry) BT17	20	A12
Glengoland Pk. (Dunmurry) BT17	20	A12
Glenhill Ct. BT14	10	F6
Glenpark St.		
Glenhill Pk. BT11	20	C11
Glenhoy Dr. BT5	17	L9
Glenhurst Gdns., New. BT36	5	H1
Glenlea Gro. BT4	13	O6
Garnerville Rd.		
Glenlea Pk. BT4	13	O6
Glenloch Gdns. BT4	13	O5
Glenluce Dr. BT4	13	O6
Glenluce Grn. BT4	13	O6
Glenluce Wk. BT4	13	O6
Glenmachan Av. BT4	19	P7
Glenmachan Dr. BT4	19	P7
Glenmachan Gro. BT4	18	O7
Glenmachan Ms. BT4	13	O6
Glenmachan Pk. BT4	13	P6
Glenmachan Pl. BT12	21	F10
Glenmachan Rd. BT4	13	O6
Glenmachan St. BT12	21	F10
Glenmillan Dr. BT4	13	O6
Glenmillan Pk. BT4	13	O6
Glenmore St. BT5	17	K8
Glenmurry Ct. BT11	20	C10
Glen Rd.		
Glenpark Ct. BT14	10	F6
Glenpark St.		
Glenpark St. BT14	10	F6
Glenravel St. BT15	16	H7
Henry Pl.		
Glenrosa Link BT15	10	H6
Glenrosa St.		
Glenrosa St. BT15	10	H6
Glenrosa St. S. BT15	10	H6
Glenshane Gdns. BT11	20	C11
Duncairn Gdns.		
Glensharragh Av. BT6	24	M11
Glensharragh Gdns. BT6	24	M11
Glensharragh Pk. BT6	24	M11
Glenside BT6	23	L12
Glenside Dr. BT14	9	D5
Glenside Par. BT14	9	D5
Glenside Pk. BT14	9	D5
Glenties Dr. BT11	20	A12
Glentilt St. BT13	15	G7
Glentoran Pl. BT6	17	K9
Mount St. S.		
Glentoran St. BT6	17	K9
Mount St. S.		
Glenvale St. BT13	15	E7
Glenvarloch St. BT5	17	L9
Glenveagh Dr. BT11	20	A11
Glenview Av. BT5	24	N11
Glenview Av., Hol. BT18	7	R3
Glenview Ct. BT5	10	F6
Glenview St.		
Glenview Cres. BT5	24	N11
Glenview Dr. BT5	24	N11
Glenview Gdns.		
Glenview Gdns. BT5	24	N11
Glenview Heights BT5	24	N11
Glenview Pk. BT5	24	N11
Glenview Rd., Hol. BT18	7	R3

Street	Page	Grid
Glenview St. BT14	10	F6
Glenview Ter. BT11	20	A12
Glenwherry Pl. BT6	17	K9
Mount St. S.		
Glenwood Pl. BT13	15	F7
Glenwood St.		
Glenwood St. BT13	15	F7
Gloucester St. BT1	16	H8
Gordon St. BT1	16	H7
Gortfin St. BT12	15	E8
Gortgrib Dr. BT5	25	Q10
Gortin Dr. BT5	19	P9
Gortin Pk. BT5	19	P9
Gortland Av. BT5	25	P10
Gortland Pk. BT5	25	P10
Gortnamona Ct. BT11	20	C10
Gortnamona Way		
Gortnamona Heights BT11	20	C10
Gortnamona Way		
Gortnamona Pl. BT11	20	C10
Gortnamona Way		
Gortnamona Ri. BT11	20	C10
Gortnamona Way		
Gortnamona Vw. BT11	20	C10
Gortnamona Way		
Gortnamona Way BT11	20	C10
Gotha St. BT6	17	K9
Governor's Bri., The BT7	22	H11
Governor's Bri., The BT9	22	H11
Grace Av. BT5	17	L9
Grace St. BT2	16	H9
Gracehill Ct. BT14	10	F6
Grafton St. BT13	15	F7
Beresford St.		
Graham Gdns. BT6	23	L10
Grampian Av. BT4	17	L8
Grampian Clo. BT4	17	L8
Grand Par. BT5	24	L10
Grange, The BT4	18	O7
Grangeville Dr. BT10	21	D13
Grangeville Gdns.		
Grangeville Gdns. BT10	20	C13
Gransha Av. BT11	20	C10
Gransha Clo. BT11	20	C10
Gransha Cres. BT11	20	C10
Gransha Dr. BT11	20	C10
Gransha Gdns. BT11	20	C10
Gransha Grn. BT11	20	C10
Gransha Gro. BT11	20	C10
Gransha Par. BT11	20	C10
Gransha Pk. BT11	20	C10
Gransha Ri. BT11	20	C10
Gransha Way BT11	20	C10
Granton Pk. BT5	19	Q9
Granville Pl. BT12	15	G8
Servia St.		
Grasmere Gdns. BT15	4	G3
Graymount Cres., New. BT36	5	H1
Graymount Dr., New. BT36	5	H2
Graymount Gdns., New. BT36	5	H1
Graymount Gro., New. BT36	5	H2
Graymount Par., New. BT36	5	H2
Graymount Pk., New. BT36	5	H2
Graymount Rd., New. BT36	5	H1
Graymount Ter., New. BT36	5	H2
Grays Ct. BT15	5	H2
Grays La. BT15	5	H2
Grays La., Hol. BT18	7	P2
High St.		
Great Georges St. BT15	16	H7
Great Northern St. BT9	22	F11
Great Patrick St. BT1	16	H7
Great Victoria St. BT2	16	H8
Green, The, Hol. BT18	7	P3
Green Av. BT11	20	B11
Green Cres. BT5	18	O9
Green Mt. BT5	24	N11
Green Rd. BT5	18	O9
Greenan BT11	20	B11
Rossnareen Rd.		
Greenane Cres. BT10	20	B13
Greenane Dr. BT10	20	B13
Greencastle BT15	10	H4
Shore Rd.		
Greencastle Clo., New. BT36	5	J1
Greencastle Pl. BT15	5	H2
Greenhill Gro. BT14	9	D4
Wolfend Dr.		
Greenhill La. BT14	9	D4
Greenland St. BT13	16	G7
Greenlea Gdns. BT5	24	N10
Whincroft Rd.		
Greenmount Pl. BT15	10	H6
Glenrosa St.		
Greenmount St. BT15	10	H6
North Queen St.		
Grenore St. BT6	17	K9
Greenville Av. BT5	17	L9
Greenville Rd. BT5	17	L9
Greenville St. BT5	17	L9
Greenway BT6	23	K11
North Bk.		
Greenwood Av. BT4	18	N8
Greenwood Manor BT4	18	N8
Greenwood Av.		
Greenwood Pk. BT4	18	O8
Gresham St. BT1	16	H8
Grey Castle Manor BT6	24	N12
Grillagh Way BT6	23	K11
Groomsport Ct. BT14	10	G6
Groomsport St.		
Groomsport St. BT14	10	G6
Grosvenor Arc. BT12	15	F9
Roden Pas.		
Grosvenor Ct. BT12	15	F9
Selby Ct.		

Street	Page	Grid
Grosvenor Rd. BT12	15	F8
Grove, The, Hol. BT18	7	P3
Grove St. E. BT5	17	L9
Grove Tree N. BT12	15	G8
Devonshire St.		
Grove Tree S. BT12	15	G8
Devonshire St.		
Grovefield Pl. BT6	17	K9
Grovefield St.		
Grovefield St. BT6	17	K9
Haddington Gdns. BT6	23	K10
Haddow St. BT13	15	F8
Sugarfield St.		
Haig St. BT5	17	K9
Halcombe St. BT6	17	K9
Hallidays Rd. BT15	10	G6
Halstein Dr. BT5	18	N9
Hamel Dr. BT6	23	L11
Hamill St. BT12	16	G8
Hamilton Pl. BT6	17	K9
Swift St.		
Hamilton Rd. BT3	17	K7
Hamilton St. BT2	16	H8
Hamiltons Ct. BT1	16	H8
High St.		
Hamlets, The BT4	18	O8
Hampton Ct., Hol. BT18	7	R2
Hampton Dr. BT7	22	H11
Hampton Gdns. BT7	22	H11
Hampton Dr.		
Hampton Gro. BT7	22	H11
Hampton Par.		
Hampton Manor BT7	23	J12
Hampton Manor Dr. BT7	23	J12
Hampton Par. BT7	22	H11
Hampton Pk. BT7	23	J13
Hampton Pl. BT7	22	H11
Hampton Dr.		
Hampton Strand BT7	22	H11
Hampton Dr.		
Hanna St. BT15	10	H6
Harberton Av. BT9	21	E13
Harberton Dr. BT9	21	E13
Harberton Pk. BT9	21	E13
Harcourt St. BT14	10	G6
Hardcastle St. BT7	16	H9
Harding Pl. BT15	10	H6
New Lo. Rd.		
Harkness Par. BT4	17	L7
Harland Pk. BT4	17	M8
Harland Rd. BT3	11	K6
Harland Wk. BT4	17	K8
Pitt Pl.		
Harleston St. BT9	22	H12
Harmony St. BT4	9	D5
Glenbank Dr.		
Harmony St. BT2	16	H9
Harper St. BT5	17	K8
Harpers St. BT1	16	H7
Curtis St.		
Harrisburg St. BT15	10	H5
Harrison Wk. BT13	10	F6
Geoffrey St.		
Harrogate St. BT12	15	F8
Harrow St. BT7	22	H10
Harrybrook St. BT13	15	F7
Hart St. BT5	17	L8
Hartington St. BT7	16	H9
Dublin Rd.		
Hartwell Pl. BT15	16	H7
Henry St.		
Harvey Ct. BT5	17	K8
Harvey St. BT5	17	K8
Hatfield St. BT7	23	J10
Hatton Dr. BT6	17	K9
Havana Ct. BT14	9	F6
Havana Gdns. BT14	9	F6
Ardoyne Av.		
Havana Wk. BT14	9	F6
Ardoyne Av.		
Havana Way BT14	9	F6
Ardoyne Av.		
Havelock St. BT7	16	H9
Ormeau Rd.		
Hawthorn St. BT12	15	F8
Hawthornden Ct. BT4	18	O8
Hawthornden Dr. BT4	18	O8
Hawthornden Gdns. BT4	18	O8
Hawthornden Ms. BT4	18	O8
Hawthornden Pk. BT4	18	O8
Hawthornden Rd. BT4	18	O8
Hawthornden Way BT4	18	O8
Haypark Av. BT7	23	J12
Haypark Gdns. BT7	23	J12
Haywood Av. BT7	22	H11
Haywood Dr. BT7	22	H11
Hazelbrook Dr. BT14	9	D4
Hazelfield St. BT13	15	F7
Crimea St.		
Hazelnut St. BT14	10	G6
Heart St. BT7	22	H10
Heather St. BT13	15	F7
Heatherbell St. BT5	17	L9
Heathfield Ct. BT14	10	F5
Torrens Rd.		
Heathfield Dr. BT14	10	F5
Heathfield Rd. BT14	10	F5
Hector St. BT5	16	H7
Helens Lea BT5	25	P10
Helgor Pk. BT4	18	N7
Helgor Pk. Ms. BT4	18	N7
Hemp St. BT5	17	K8
Newtownards Rd.		
Hemsworth St. BT13	15	G7
Agnes St.		

Street	Page	Grid
Henderson Av. BT15	4	G3
Henderson Av. Flats BT15	4	G3
Henderson Ct. BT15	4	G3
Henderson Av.		
Henderson Ct., Hol. BT18	13	O5
Henrietta St. BT2	16	H9
Henry Pl. BT15	16	H7
Henry Sq. BT1	16	H7
Exchange St.		
Henry St. BT15	16	H7
Henryville St. BT6	17	K9
Shamrock St.		
Herat St. BT7	22	H11
Delhi St.		
Herbert St. BT14	9	E6
Herdman Channel Rd. BT3	11	K5
Heron Av. BT3	6	N3
Heron Rd. BT3	6	N3
Herrons Row BT13	15	F7
Beresford St.		
Hertford St. BT12	15	F8
Grosvenor Rd.		
Hesketh Gdns. BT14	9	E5
Hesketh Pk. BT14	9	E5
Hesketh Rd. BT14	9	E5
Hewitt Par. BT5	18	N9
Hibernia St., Hol. BT18	7	P2
High Link BT13	14	D8
High Pass BT13	14	D8
High Side BT13	14	D8
High St. BT1	16	H8
High St., Hol. BT18	7	P2
High St. Ct. BT1	16	H8
Victoria St.		
High St. La. BT1	16	H8
High St.		
Highburn Cres. BT13	14	D7
Highburn Gdns. BT13	14	D7
Highbury Gdns. BT14	9	E6
Highcairn Dr. BT13	14	D7
Highcliff Gdns. BT13	14	D7
Highdene Gdns. BT13	14	D7
Highfern Gdns. BT13	14	D7
Highfield Dr. BT13	14	D8
Highgate BT13	14	D7
West Circular Rd.		
Highgate Ter. BT13	14	D7
Highfield Dr.		
Highgreen BT13	14	D7
Highland Par. BT13	14	D7
Highpark Cres. BT13	14	D8
Highpark Cross BT13	14	D8
Highpark Dr. BT13	14	D7
Highvale Gdns. BT13	14	D7
Highview Cres. BT13	14	D7
Highway BT13	14	D7
Hill St. BT1	16	H7
Hillburn Pk. BT6	24	M11
Hillcrest Gdns. BT5	17	M9
Hillfoot St. BT4	17	M8
Hillhead Av. BT11	20	B12
Hillhead Ct. BT11	20	B12
Hillhead Cres. BT11	20	B12
Hillhead Dr. BT11	20	B12
Hillhead Heights BT11	20	B12
Hillhead Pk. BT11	20	B12
Hillman St. BT15	10	H6
Hills Av. BT4	17	L7
Hillsborough Dr. BT6	23	K10
Hillsborough Gdns. BT6	23	L10
Hillsborough Par. BT6	23	L10
Hillside Cres. BT9	22	G12
Hillside Dr. BT9	22	G12
Hillside Gdns. BT9	22	G12
Hillside Pk. BT9	22	G12
Hillview Av. BT5	18	N9
Hillview Ct. BT14	10	F6
Ewarts Pl.		
Hillview Pl., Hol. BT18	7	Q2
Hillview Rd. BT14	10	F6
Hind St. BT5	17	L8
Hindsdale Pk. BT6	23	L12
Hogarth St. BT15	10	H6
Holland Cres. BT5	18	N9
Holland Dr. BT5	18	N9
Holland Gdns. BT5	18	N9
Holland Pk. BT5	18	N9
Hollycroft Av. BT5	17	L9
Holmdene Gdns. BT14	9	E6
Holmes St. BT1	16	J8
Verner St.		
Holmes St. BT2	16	H9
Holyrood BT9	22	G11
Holywood Bypass, Hol. BT18	7	P3
Holywood Rd. BT4	17	M8
Holywood Rd., Hol. BT18	13	O5
Hope Ct. BT12	16	H9
Hope St.		
Hope St. BT12	16	G9
Hopedene Ct. BT4	18	M8
Dundela Gdns.		
Hopedene Ms. BT4	18	M8
Dundela Av.		
Hopefield Av. BT15	10	G5
Hopewell Av. BT13	15	G7
Hopewell Cres. BT13	15	G7
Hopewell Pl. BT13	15	G7
Hopewell Sq. BT13	15	G7
Horn Dr. BT11	20	A12
Horn Wk. BT11	20	A12
Hornby Cres. BT5	17	L8
Hornby Par. BT5	17	L8
Hornby St.		
Hornby St. BT5	17	L8
Horseshoe Row BT14	9	D4
Houston Ct. BT5	18	N8
Houston Dr. BT5	24	M10

Ladymar Gro. BT12 15 G8
Lady St.
Ladymar Pk. BT12 15 G8
Lady St.
Ladymar Wk. BT12 15 G8
Lady St.
Ladymar St. BT12 15 G8
Ladymar Way BT12 15 G8
Lady St.
Lagan Bk. Rd. BT1 16 J8
Lagan Bri. BT1 16 J7
Lagan Bri. BT3 16 J7
Lagan La. BT7 16 J8
Verner St.
Laganvale Ct. BT9 22 H12
Laganvale Manor BT9 22 H12
Laganvale St. BT9 22 H12
Laganview Ct. BT5 16 J8
Laganview Ms. BT5 16 J8
Lake Glen Av. BT11 21 D10
Lake Glen Clo. BT11 21 D10
Lake Glen Cres. BT11 21 D10
Lake Glen Dr. BT11 21 D10
Lake Glen Grn. BT11 21 D10
Lake Glen Par. BT11 21 D10
Lake Glen Dr.
Lake Glen Pk. BT11 21 D10
Lake St. BT7 16 H9
Lanark St. BT13 15 E8
Lanark Way BT13 15 E8
Lancaster St. BT15 16 H7
Lancedean Rd. BT6 24 L12
Lancefield Rd. BT9 21 F12
Landscape Ter. BT14 10 G6
Landseer St. BT9 22 H10
Langholm Row BT5 19 Q9
Granton Pk.
Langley St. BT13 15 F7
Tennent St.
Lansdowne Dr. BT15 5 H3
Lansdowne Pk. BT15 5 H3
Lansdowne Pk. N. BT15 5 H3
Lansdowne Rd. BT15 5 H3
Lanyon Pl. BT1 16 J8
Larch Clo., Hol. BT18 7 P3
Loughview Av.
Larch St. BT5 17 K9
Trillick St.
Larkfield Ct. BT4 18 M7
Larkfield Rd.
Larkfield Dr. BT4 17 M7
Larkfield Gdns. BT4 17 M7
Larkfield Gro. BT4 17 M7
Larkfield Manor BT4 17 M7
Larkfield Pk. BT4 18 M7
Larkfield Rd. BT4 17 M7
Larkstone St. BT9 21 F12
Lisburn Rd.
Laurel Wd. BT8 23 J13
Laurelvale BT4 18 N8
Lavens Dr. BT14 9 D5
Lawnbrook Av. BT13 15 F8
Lawnbrook Dr. BT13 15 F7
Lawnbrook Av.
Lawnbrook Sq. BT13 15 F7
Lawnbrook Av.
Lawnmount St. BT6 17 K9
Lawnview St. BT13 15 E7
Lawrence St. BT7 22 H10
Laws Ct. BT1 16 H7
Lawther Ct. BT15 10 H6
Lawther St. BT15 10 H6
Lawyer Gdns. BT12 16 G9
Linfield Rd.
Lead Hill BT6 24 N11
Lead Hill Pk. BT6 24 N11
Lead Hill Vw. BT6 24 N11
Lecale St. BT12 21 F10
Lecumpher St. BT5 17 L9
Ledley Hall Clo. BT5 17 L8
Avoniel Rd.
Leeson St. BT12 15 F8
Leestone Ter. BT11 20 B12
Kells Av.
Legann St. BT14 9 D5
Leganoe St. BT14 8 C4
Legboy St. BT14 8 C4
Ligoniel Rd.
Leggagh Ct. BT14 9 D4
Leginn St. BT14 9 D4
Legmail St. BT14 9 E5
Crumlin Rd.
Legmore St. BT14 8 C4
Ligoniel Rd.
Legnavea Pl. BT14 8 C4
Leganoe St.
Legnavea St. BT14 8 C4
Legoniel Pl. BT14 8 C4
Leitrim St. BT6 17 K9
Lelia St. BT4 17 L8
Lemberg St. BT12 15 F9
Lemon St. BT12 15 F8
Ross St.
Lemonfield Av., Hol. BT18 7 Q3
Lena St. BT5 17 L8
Lenadoon Av. BT11 20 A11
Lenadoon Wk. BT11 20 A12
Lendrick St. BT5 17 K8
Lennoxvale BT9 22 G11
Leopold Pl. BT13 9 F6
Leopold St. BT13 15 F7
Leoville St. BT13 15 F8
Lepper St. BT15 10 H6
Leroy St. BT14 9 D5
Leven Clo. BT5 19 Q10
Leven Dr.
Leven Cres. BT5 19 Q10
Leven Dr. BT5 19 Q10

Leven Pk. BT5 19 Q10
Leven Pl. BT5 19 Q10
Leven Dr.
Lever St. BT14 8 C4
Lewis St. BT15 10 H6
Library Ct. BT4 18 N8
Library St. BT1 16 H7
Lichfield Av. BT5 17 M9
Liffey Ct. BT14 10 G6
Shannon St.
Ligoniel Pl. BT14 8 C4
Wolfhill La.
Ligoniel Rd. BT14 8 C3
Lilliput Ct. BT15 10 H6
Clanmorris St.
Lilliput St. BT15 10 H6
Lime Ct. BT13 16 G7
Limegrove BT15 5 H2
Limehill Gro. BT14 9 D4
Leginn St.
Limehill St. BT14 9 D4
Limepark Ms. BT14 9 D5
Lavens Dr.
Limepark St. BT14 9 D5
Lavens Dr.
Limestone Rd. BT15 10 G5
Limewood Gro. BT4 18 N8
Kincora Av.
Lincoln Av. BT14 10 G6
Lincoln Pl. BT12 16 H9
Lincoln Sq. BT12 15 F8
Abyssinia St.
Lincoln St. BT12 15 F8
Linden Gdns. BT14 10 G5
Linden St. BT13 15 F8
Falls Rd.
Lindsay Ct. BT7 16 H9
Lindsay St.
Lindsay St. BT7 16 H9
Lindsay Way BT7 16 H9
Lindsay St.
Linen Gro. BT14 9 D4
Linen Hall St. BT2 16 H8
Linen Hall St. W. BT2 16 H9
Linfield Av. BT12 16 G9
Linfield Rd.
Linfield Dr. BT12 16 G9
Linfield Rd.
Linfield Gdns. BT12 16 G9
Linfield Rd.
Linfield Rd. BT12 16 G9
Linfield St. BT12 16 G9
Linfield Rd.
Linview Ct. BT12 15 F9
Roden St.
Lisavon Dr. BT4 17 M7
Lisavon Par. BT4 17 M7
Lisavon St. BT4 17 M7
Lisbon St. BT5 17 K8
Lisburn Av. BT9 22 F11
Lisburn Rd. BT9 22 F11
Lisdarragh Pk. BT14 4 F3
Lisfaddan Cres. BT12 15 G8
Lisfaddan Dr. BT12 15 G8
Milford St.
Lisfaddan Pl. BT12 15 G8
Milford St.
Lisfaddan Way BT12 16 G8
Lislea Av. BT9 21 F12
Lisburn Rd.
Lislea Dr. BT9 21 E12
Lisleen Rd. BT5 25 P12
Lismain St. BT6 23 K10
Lismore St. BT6 17 K9
Lismoyne Pk. BT15 4 G3
Lisnasharragh Pk. BT6 24 M11
Lisnasharragh Rd. BT6 24 M11
Lisnasharragh Ter. BT6 24 M11
Lisnasharragh Pk.
Lissan Clo. BT6 23 K12
Lissan Link BT6 23 K12
Lissan Clo.
Lisvarna Heights BT12 15 F8
Lisvarna Pl. BT12 15 F8
Lisburn Rd.
Little Brunswick St. BT2 16 H9
Little Charlotte St. BT7 16 H9
Charlotte St.
Little Corporation St. BT15 16 J7
Corporation St.
Little Donegall St. BT1 16 H7
Little Edward St. BT1 16 H7
Edward St.
Little Georges St. BT15 16 H7
Henry St.
Little Grosvenor St. BT12 15 G9
Burnaby Pl.
Little Henry St. BT15 16 H7
Henry St.
Little May St. BT2 16 H8
Little Patrick St. BT15 16 H7
Little Victoria St. BT2 16 H9
Little York St. BT15 16 H7
Locan St. BT12 15 E9
Lochinver Dr. BT10 19 Q9
Locksley Dr. BT10 21 D13
Locksley Pk. BT10 21 D13
Lockview Ct. BT9 22 H12
Lockview Rd. BT9 22 H11
Lombard St. BT1 16 H8
Rosemary St.
Lomond Av. BT4 17 M8
Lomond St. BT4 17 M8
London Rd. BT6 17 K9
London St. BT6 17 K9
Longacre BT8 23 J13
Loopland Cres. BT6 23 L10
Loopland Dr. BT6 23 L10

Loopland Gdns. BT6 23 L10
Loopland Gro. BT6 23 L10
Loopland Par. BT6 23 L10
Loopland Pk.
Loopland Pk. BT6 23 L10
Loopland Rd. BT6 23 L10
Lord St. BT5 17 K9
Lorne St. BT9 22 F10
Lothair Av. BT15 10 G5
Lothian Av. BT5 25 Q10
Louden St. BT13 15 G7
Lough Lea BT5 16 J8
Loughrey Ct. BT15 10 G5
Loughview Av., Hol. BT18 7 P3
Loughview Dr. BT6 23 K13
Loughview St. BT14 9 D4
Crumlin Rd.
Loughview Ter. BT15 10 H5
Louisa Ct. BT14 10 F6
Ardilea St.
Louisa St. BT14 10 F6
Lovatt St. BT5 17 L8
Ravenscroft Av.
Lower Braniel Rd. BT5 24 N11
Lower California St. BT13 15 G7
Old Lo. Rd.
Lower Clara Cres. BT5 17 L9
Clara Av.
Lower Clonard St. BT12 15 F8
Lower Cres. BT7 16 H9
Lower Garfield St. BT1 16 H8
Lower Kilburn St. BT12 15 F9
Lower Lo. Av. BT14 9 E4
Oldpark Rd.
Lower Mt. St. BT5 17 K9
Mount St.
Lower Regent St. BT13 16 H7
Lower Rockview St. BT12 15 F9
Lower Stanfield St. BT7 16 J9
Lower Urney St. BT13 15 F8
Lower Windsor Av. BT9 22 F10
Lowland Av. BT5 18 O9
Lowland Gdns. BT5 19 Q9
Lowland Av.
Lowland Wk. BT5 19 Q10
Kilmory Gdns.
Lowry St. BT5 17 K8
Lowwood Gdns. BT15 5 H3
Lowwood Pk. BT15 5 H3
Lucerne Par. BT9 22 H12
Lucknow St. BT13 15 F8
Ludlow Sq. BT15 10 H6
Lupus Gro. BT14 9 D4
Luxor Gdns. BT5 17 M9
Lyle St. BT13 15 G7
Lyndhurst Clo. BT13 14 D7
Lyndhurst Dr. BT13 9 D6
Lyndhurst Gdns. BT13 14 D7
Lyndhurst Gro. BT13 14 D7
Lyndhurst Link BT13 14 D7
Lyndhurst Par. BT13 14 D7
Lyndhurst Pk. BT13 14 D7
Lyndhurst Ri. BT13 14 D7
Lyndhurst Way BT13 14 D7
Lynmouth St. BT12 15 E8
Clovelly St.
Lynwood Pk., Hol. BT18 7 Q3

Mabel Ct. BT12 15 G9
Mabel St. BT12 15 G9
Utility St.
Macart Rd. BT3 16 J7
Mackey St. BT15 10 H6
Madison Av. BT15 10 G4
Madison Av. E. BT4 17 L8
Madras St. BT13 15 F7
Madrid Ct. BT5 17 K8
Madrid St.
Madrid St. BT5 17 K8
Magdala St. BT7 22 H10
Magees La. BT15 16 H7
Maghies Pl. BT6 17 K9
Pearl St.
Main St., New. BT36 5 J1
Majestic Dr. BT12 16 G9
Major St. BT5 17 K8
Malcolmson St. BT13 15 F8
Maldon St. BT12 15 F9
Malinmore Pk. BT11 20 B12
Malmouth St. BT12 14 D8
Springfield Rd.
Malone Av. BT9 22 G10
Malone Chase BT9 22 G11
Malone Ct. BT9 21 F13
Malone Ct. Ms. BT9 21 F13
Malone Ct.
Malone Pk. BT9 22 F13
Malone Pk. BT9 21 E12
Malone Pk. Cen. BT9 21 F13
Malone Pk. La. BT9 21 E12
Malone Pl. BT12 16 G9
Malone Rd. BT9 22 G11
Malvern Clo. BT13 15 G7
Malvern Pl. BT13 15 G7
Malvern St.
Malvern St. BT13 15 G7
Malvern Way BT13 15 G7
Manderson St. BT4 17 L8
Manilla St. BT14 9 F6
Manna Gro. BT5 24 M10
Mann's Rd. BT5 25 Q12
Manor Ct. BT14 10 G6
Manor Dr. BT14 10 G6
Manor St. BT14 10 G6
Manse Rd. BT6 24 M13

Mansfield St. BT13   15   G7
Downing St.
Maple Ct., Hol. BT18   7   P3
Loughview Av.
Mara Gdns., Hol. BT18   7   Q2
Strand Av.
Maralin Pl. BT15   10   H6
Sheridan St.
March St. BT13   15   E7
Marchioness Grn. BT12   15   G8
Marchioness St.
Marchioness St. BT12   15   G8
Marcus Ward St. BT7   16   H9
Marfield St. BT4   17   K8
St. Leonards St.
Margaretta Pk. (Dunmurry) BT17   20   A13
Marguerite Pk. BT10   21   D13
Marina Pk. BT5   24   M10
Marine Par., Hol. BT18   7   P2
Marine St. BT15   11   J6
Marino Pk., Hol. BT18   7   R1
Market St. BT1   16   H8
Market St. BT7   16   H9
Marlborough Av. BT9   21   F11
Lisburn Av.
Marlborough Ct. BT1   16   H8
Princes St.
Marlborough Ct. BT9   21   F11
Lisburn Rd.
Marlborough Gdns. BT9   22   F12
Marlborough Heights BT6   24   N11
Marlborough Pk. BT9   22   G11
Malone Rd.
Marlborough Pk. Cen. BT9   22   F11
Marlborough Pk. Cross Av. BT9   22   F11
Marlborough Pk. N. BT9   22   F11
Marlborough Pk. S. BT9   22   F11
Marlborough St. BT1   16   H8
Marlfield Dr. BT5   25   O10
Marlfield Ri. BT5   25   O10
Marmont Cres. BT4   12   N6
Marmont Dr. BT4   12   N6
Marmont Pk. BT4   12   N6
Marmount Gdns. BT14   9   E4
Marquis St. BT1   16   H8
Marsden Gdns. BT15   10   G5
Marsden Gdns. Flats BT15   10   G5
Marsden Gdns.
Marsden Ter. BT15   10   G5
Marsden Gdns.
Marshall St. BT1   16   H7
Dunbar St.
Marshalls Rd. BT5   24   M11
Martello Ter., Hol. BT18   7   Q2
Martin St. BT5   17   K8
Martinez Av. BT5   17   M9
Marylebone Pk. BT9   22   H12
Maryville Av. BT9   21   F11
Maryville Ct. BT7   16   H9
Maryville St.
Maryville Pk. BT9   21   E12
Maryville St. BT7   16   H9
Mashona Ct. BT6   17   K9
Massareene Path BT12   16   G8
Cullingtree Rd.
Massareene Row BT12   16   G8
Cullingtree Rd.
Massareene Wk. BT12   16   G8
Cullingtree Rd.
Massareene Way BT12   15   G8
Divis St.
Massey Av. BT4   19   P7
Massey Ct. BT4   19   P7
Massey Grn. BT4   18   O7
Massey Pk. BT4   19   P7
Matchett St. BT13   15   F7
Matilda Av. BT12   16   G9
Blythe St.
Matilda Dr. BT12   16   G9
Blythe St.
Matilda Gdns. BT12   15   G9
Mabel St.
Matilda St. BT12   15   G9
Bentham Dr.
Maurice Ter. BT12   15   E7
Mawhinneys Ct. BT13   16   G8
Melbourne St.
Maxwell St. BT12   16   G9
Maxwells Pl. BT12   16   G9
Aughrin Pk.
May St. BT1   16   H8
Mayfair Av. BT6   23   L11
Mayfair Ct. BT14   10   F6
Ardilea St.
Mayfield St. BT9   21   F11
Mayflower St. BT5   17   L9
Maymount St. BT6   17   K9
Mayo Ct. BT13   15   F7
Mayo Link BT13   15   E7
Mayo St.
Mayo Pl. BT13   15   F7
Mayo St. BT13   15   E7
Mays Mkt. BT1   16   J8
Oxford St.
Mays Meadow BT1   16   J8
McAdam Gdns. BT12   16   G9
Linfield Rd.
McAdam Pk. BT12   16   G9
McAllister St. BT4   17   L8
Mersey St.
McArthur Ct. BT4   17   K8
McAuley Ct. BT7   16   H9
McAuley St.
McAuley St. BT7   16   H9
McCandless St. BT13   15   F7

McCaughan Pk. BT6   24   L12
McCaughey Rd. BT3   11   J6
McCavanas Pl. BT2   16   H9
McCavanas St.
McCavanas St. BT2   16   H9
McCleery St. BT15   16   H7
North Hill St.
McClintock St. BT2   16   H9
McClure St. BT7   16   H9
McDonnell Ct. BT12   15   G8
Servia St.
McDonnell St. BT12   15   G8
McDowells Row BT14   8   C3
Ligoniel Rd.
McDowells Row BT15   10   H4
Shore Rd.
McDowells Row, New. BT36   5   J2
Shore Rd.
McFarlands Ct. BT12   15   E9
Donegall Rd.
McGahan St. BT12   16   G9
Linfield Rd.
McIvors Pl. BT13   15   G8
Brown St.
McKibbens Ct. BT1   16   H7
North St.
McMaster St. BT5   17   K8
McMullans La. BT6   16   J9
McQuillan St. BT13   15   F8
Colligan St.
Meadowbank Pl. BT9   22   F10
Meadowbank St. BT9   22   F11
Medway Ct. BT4   17   K8
Medway St.
Medway St. BT4   17   K8
Meekon St. BT4   17   L8
Melbourne Ct. BT13   16   G8
Melbourne St.
Melbourne St. BT13   16   G8
Melfort Dr. BT5   25   Q10
Melrose Av. BT5   17   L9
Melrose St. BT9   22   F10
Meridi St. BT12   15   F9
Merkland Pl. BT13   15   E7
Merkland St. BT13   15   E8
Merok Cres. BT6   24   L11
Merok Dr. BT6   24   L11
Merok Gdns. BT6   24   L11
Merok Pk. BT6   24   L11
Merrion St. BT12   15   F8
Merryfield Dr. BT15   4   G3
Mersey St. BT4   17   L8
Mertoun Pk. BT4   13   O5
Mervue Ct. BT15   10   H6
Mervue St. BT15   10   H6
Meyrick Ter. BT14   9   E4
Mica Dr. BT12   15   E8
Mica St. BT12   15   E9
Middle Braniel Rd. BT5   25   O12
Middlepath St. BT5   16   J8
Midland Clo. BT15   10   H6
Midland Cres. BT15   10   H6
Midland Clo.
Mileriver St. BT15   10   H5
Milewater Basin BT3   11   J6
Milewater Rd. BT3   11   J5
Milewater St. BT15   10   H6
Milford Pl. BT12   15   G8
Milford Ri. BT12   15   G8
Milford St.
Milford St. BT12   15   G8
Milk St. BT5   17   L8
Bloomfield Av.
Mill Av. BT14   8   C4
Mill St. W. BT13   15   F7
Millar St. BT6   23   K10
Millbank Pk. BT14   9   D4
Wolfend Dr.
Millfield BT1   16   G8
Milliken St. BT12   15   F8
Ross St.
Milltown Row BT12   21   D10
Millview Ct. BT14   9   D4
Milner St. BT12   15   F9
Mineral St. BT15   10   H5
Mizen Gdns. BT11   20   B12
Moffatt St. BT5   16   H7
Moira Ct. BT5   17   K8
Moira St. BT5   17   K8
Moltke St. BT12   15   F9
Molyneaux St. BT15   16   H7
Henry St.
Monagh Cres. BT11   14   C9
Monagh Dr. BT11   14   C9
Monagh Gro. BT11   14   C9
Monagh Link BT11   20   C10
Monagh Par. BT11   14   C9
Monagh Rd. BT11   20   C10
Monagh Rd. Bypass BT11   14   C9
Monarch Par. BT12   15   F9
Monarch St. BT12   15   F9
Moneyrea St. BT6   17   K9
Montgomery Ct. BT6   24   L11
Montgomery Rd. BT6   23   L11
Montgomery St. BT1   16   H8
Montreal St. BT13   9   E6
Montrose St. BT5   17   K8
Montrose St. S. BT5   17   K8
Montrose Wk. BT5   17   K8
Montrose St.
Moonstone St. BT9   21   F11
Moor Pk. Av. BT10   20   B13
Moor Pk. Dr. BT10   20   B13
Moor Pk. Gdns. BT10   20   B13
Moor Pk. Ms. BT10   20   B13
Mooreland Cres. BT11   21   D12
Mooreland Dr. BT11   21   D11

Mooreland Pk. BT11   21   D11
Moore's Pl. BT12   16   G9
Sandy Row
Moorfield St. BT5   17   M8
Moorgate St. BT5   17   M8
Mornington BT7   23   J12
Mornington Ms. BT7   23   J12
Mornington
Morpeth St. BT13   15   G7
Tyne St.
Moscow St. BT13   15   F7
Shankill Rd.
Moss Rd., Hol. BT18   13   Q6
Moss Rd. (Redburn), Hol. BT18   13   P4
Mossvale St. BT13   15   E7
Motelands BT4   13   O6
Motelands, Hol. BT18   13   P4
Mount, The BT5   17   K9
Mount Alverno BT12   14   C9
Mount Carmel BT15   10   G4
Mount Charles BT7   22   H10
Mount Coole Gdns. BT14   4   F3
Mount Coole Pk. BT14   4   F3
Mount Eden Pk. BT9   21   F13
Mount Merrion BT6   23   K11
Mount Merrion Av. BT6   23   K12
Mount Merrion Cres. BT6   23   K12
Mount Merrion Dr. BT6   23   K12
Mount Merrion Gdns. BT6   23   K11
Mount Merrion Pk. BT6   23   K12
Mount Pleasant BT9   22   H11
Mount Prospect Pk. BT9   22   G10
Mount St. BT5   17   K9
Mount St. BT6   17   K9
Mount St. S. BT6   17   K9
Mount Vernon Dr. BT15   5   H3
Mount Vernon Gdns. BT15   5   H3
Mount Vernon Grn. BT15   10   H4
Mount Vernon Gro. BT15   10   H4
Mount Vernon Pk.
Mount Vernon La. BT15   5   H3
Mount Vernon Pk. BT15   5   H3
Mount Vernon Pas. BT15   5   H3
Mount Vernon Rd. BT15   5   H3
Mount Vernon Wk. BT15   5   H3
Mountainhill La. BT14   8   C4
Mountainhill Rd. BT14   8   C4
Mountainhill Rd.
Mountainhill Wk. BT14   8   C4
Mountainhill Rd.
Mountainview Dr. BT14   9   E6
Mountainview Gdns. BT14   9   E6
Mountainview Par. BT14   9   E6
Mountainview Pk. BT14   9   E6
Mountainview Pl. BT14   9   E6
Mountcashel St. BT13   15   E7
Mountcollyer Av. BT15   10   H6
Mountcollyer Rd. BT15   10   H5
Mountcollyer St. BT15   10   H5
Mountforde Ct. BT5   17   K8
Mountforde Dr.
Mountforde Dr. BT5   17   K8
Mountforde Gdns. BT5   17   K8
Mountforde Dr.
Mountforde Pk. BT5   17   K8
Mountforde Dr.
Mountforde Rd. BT5   17   K8
Mountjoy St. BT13   15   F7
Mountpottinger Link BT5   16   J8
Mountpottinger Rd. BT5   16   J8
Mountview Ct. BT14   10   G6
Mountview St. BT5   10   G6
Mourne St. BT5   17   L8
Mowhan St. BT9   21   F11
Moyard Cres. BT12   14   C8
Moyard Par. BT12   14   C8
Moyard Pk. BT12   14   D8
Moyne Pk. BT5   25   Q10
Moyola St. BT15   10   H6
Mulhouse Rd. BT12   15   F9
Mulroy Pk. BT11   20   A11
Murphys Ct. BT15   16   H7
Murphys La. BT7   16   H9
Market St.
Murray St. BT1   16   G8
Murrays Pl. BT6   23   J11
Ravenhill Rd.
Musgrave Channel Rd. BT3   17   K7
Musgrave Pk. Ct. BT9   21   E12
Stockmans La.
Musgrave Rd. BT3   11   K6
Musgrave St. BT1   16   H8
Ann St.
Music Hall Ct. BT1   16   H8
Music Hall La.
Music Hall La. BT1   16   H8
My Ladys Mile, Hol. BT18   7   P3
My Ladys Rd. BT6   17   K9
Myrtlefield Pk. BT9   21   E12

Nansen St. BT12   15   E9
Napier St. BT12   16   G9
Blondin St.
Naroon Pk. BT11   20   B11
Nassau St. BT13   15   F7
Beresford St.
Navan Grn. BT11   20   C11
Neely St. BT12   15   F9
Neills Hill Pk. BT5   18   N9
Nelson Pl. BT15   16   H7
Nelson St.
Nelson Sq. BT13   15   F7
Nelson St. BT15   16   H7
Nendrum Gdns. BT5   17   M9

Street			
Netherleigh Pk. BT4	19	P7
Nevis Av. BT4	17	M8
New Barnsley Cres. BT12	14	C8
New Barnsley Dr. BT12	14	C8
New Barnsley Gdns. BT12	14	D8
New Barnsley Grn. BT12	14	C8
New Barnsley Gro. BT12	14	C8
New Barnsley Par. BT12	14	C8
New Barnsley Pk. BT12	14	C8
New Bond St. BT7	16	J9
New Fm. La. BT14	9	D4
Leginn St.		
New Forge Gra. BT9	22	F13
New Lo. Pl. BT15	10	H6
New Lo. Rd.		
New Lo. Rd. BT15	10	H6
Newcastle Manor BT4	17	K8
Newcastle St.		
Newcastle St. BT4	17	K8
Newforge Dale BT9	22	F13
Newforge La. BT9	22	F13
Newington Av. BT15	10	G6
Newington St. BT15	10	H6
Newport Ct. BT14	10	G6
Newry St. BT6	17	K9
Newtownards Rd. BT4	17	K8
Norbloom Gdns. BT5	17	M9
Norbury St. BT11	21	D10
Norfolk Dr. BT11	21	D10
Norfolk Gdns. BT11	20	C10
Norfolk Gro. BT11	20	C10
Norfolk Par. BT11	21	D10
Norfolk Rd. BT11	20	C10
Norfolk Way BT11	20	C10
Norglen Ct. BT11	14	C9
Norglen Cres. BT11	20	C10
Norglen Dr. BT11	20	C10
Norglen Gdns. BT11	20	C10
Norglen Gro. BT11	14	C9
Norglen Par. BT11	14	C9
Norglen Rd. BT11	20	C10
North Av. BT15	10	G4
North Bk. BT6	23	K11
North Boundary St. BT13	16	G7
North Circular Rd. BT14	4	F3
North Circular Rd. BT15	4	F3
North Clo., Hol. BT18	7	P3
North Derby St. BT15	10	H6
North Gdns. BT5	18	M9
North Grn. BT11	20	C11
North Hill St. BT15	16	H7
North Howard Ct. BT13	15	F8
Fifth St.		
North Howard Link BT13	15	F8
North Howard St. BT13	15	F8
North Howard Wk. BT13	15	F7
North King St. BT13	16	G7
Gardiner St.		
North Link BT11	20	C11
North Par. BT7	23	J11
North Queen St. BT15	16	H7
North Rd. BT4	18	M8
North Rd. BT5	18	M9
North Sperrin BT5	19	Q9
North St. BT1	16	H7
North St. Arc. BT1	16	H7
North St.		
Northbrook Gdns. BT9	22	F10
Northbrook St. BT9	22	F10
Northern Rd. BT3	11	J6
Northfield Ri. BT5	24	N11
Northland Ct. BT13	15	F7
Northland St.		
Northland St. BT13	15	F7
Northlands Pk. BT10	20	C12
Northumberland St. BT13	15	G8
Northwick Dr. BT14	9	E5
Northwood Cres. BT15	10	H4
Northwood Dr. BT15	10	H5
Northwood Par. BT15	10	H4
Northwood Rd. BT15	10	H4
Norton St. BT9	21	F13
Norton St. BT7	16	H9
Norwood Av. BT4	18	N7
Norwood Ct. BT4	18	N7
Norwood Cres. BT4	18	N7
Norwood Dr. BT4	18	N7
Norwood Gdns. BT4	18	N7
Norwood Gro. BT4	18	N7
Norwood La., Hol. BT18	7	P3
Norwood Pk. BT4	18	N7
Norwood St. BT12	16	H9
Notting Hill BT9	22	G11
Notting Hill Ct. BT9	22	G12
Notting Hill Manor BT9	22	G12
Nubia St. BT12	15	F9
Nun's Wk., Hol. BT18	7	Q3
Oak St. BT7	16	H9
Elm St.		
Oak Way BT7	16	H9
Oakdale St. BT5	17	L8
Oakdene Dr. BT4	17	M7
Oakdene Par. BT4	17	M7
Oakland Av. BT4	18	M8
Oakley Av., Hol. BT18	7	P3
Oakley St. BT14	9	D5
Oakman St. BT12	15	E8
Oakmount Dr. BT15	11	J4
Oakwood Ct. BT9	21	F13
Oakwood Gro. BT9	21	F13
Oakwood Ms. BT9	21	F13
Oakwood Pk. BT9	21	F13
Oban St. BT12	16	G9
Oberon St. BT6	23	K10
Oceanic Av. BT15	10	G5

Street			
O'Dempsey St. BT15	11	J5
Odessa St. BT13	15	F8
Ogilvie St. BT6	23	K10
Ohio St. BT13	9	E6
Old Cavehill Rd. BT15	4	G3
Old Channel Rd. BT3	16	J7
Old Dundonald Rd.	19	R9
(Dundonald) BT16		
Old Holywood Rd. BT4	13	O6
Old Holywood Rd., Hol.	13	O5
BT18		
Old Lo. Rd. BT13	15	G7
Old Mill Rd. BT14	9	D4
Old Mill Way BT14	9	D4
Old Mill Rd.		
Old Quay Ct., Hol. BT18	7	R1
Old Quay Rd., Hol. BT18	7	R1
Old Westland Rd. BT14	4	F4
Oldpark Av. BT14	10	F6
Oldpark Rd. BT14	9	E4
Oldpark Sq. BT14	10	F6
Ardoyne Av.		
Oldpark Ter. BT14	10	F5
Olive St. BT13	15	E7
Olympia Dr. BT12	21	F10
Olympia Par. BT12	21	F10
Olympia St. BT12	22	F10
Omeath St. BT6	17	K9
O'Neill St. BT13	15	F8
O'Neills Pl., Hol. BT18	7	Q2
Church Vw.		
Onslow Gdns. BT6	23	K11
Onslow Par. BT6	23	K11
Onslow Pk. BT6	23	K11
Ophir Gdns. BT15	10	G4
Orangefield Av. BT5	18	M9
Orangefield Cres. BT6	24	L10
Orangefield Dr. BT5	18	M9
Orangefield Dr. S. BT5	18	M9
Orangefield Gdns. BT5	18	M9
Orangefield Grn. BT5	18	M9
Orangefield Gro. BT5	18	M9
Orangefield La. BT5	18	M9
Orangefield Par. BT5	18	M9
Orangefield Pk. BT5	18	M9
Orangefield Rd. BT5	18	M9
Oranmore Dr. BT11	20	B13
Oranmore St. BT13	15	F8
Orby Dr. BT5	24	L10
Orby Gdns. BT5	24	L10
Orby Grn. BT5	24	L10
Orby Gro. BT5	24	M10
Orby Link BT5	24	L10
Orby Ms. BT5	24	M10
Orby Par. BT5	24	L10
Orby Pk. BT5	24	L10
Orby Pl. BT5	24	M10
Orby Rd. BT5	17	L9
Orby St. BT5	24	M10
Orchard Clo. BT5	25	O10
Orchard St. BT15	10	H6
Canning St.		
Orchardvale BT6	24	M12
Orchardville Av. BT10	20	C12
Orchardville Cres. BT10	20	C13
Orchardville Gdns. BT10	21	D13
Oregon Gdns. BT13	15	F7
Orient Gdns. BT14	10	G5
Orkney St. BT13	15	F7
Ormeau Av. BT2	16	H9
Ormeau Bri. BT7	23	J10
Ormeau Embk. BT6	23	J10
Ormeau Embk. BT7	23	J10
Ormeau Rd. BT7	16	H9
Ormeau St. BT7	16	H9
Ormiston Cres. BT4	18	O8
Ormiston Dr. BT4	18	O8
Ormiston Gdns. BT4	18	O9
Ormiston Par. BT4	18	O8
Ormiston Pk. BT4	18	O8
Ormond Pl. BT12	15	G8
Roumania Ri.		
Ormonde Gdns. BT6	23	L10
Orrs Entry BT1	16	H8
High St.		
Osborne Dr. BT9	21	F12
Osborne Gdns. BT9	21	F12
Osborne Pk. BT9	21	F12
Osman St. BT12	15	F8
Oswald Pk. BT12	15	G9
Ottawa St. BT13	9	F7
Outram St. BT7	16	H9
Oval St. BT4	17	L8
Owenvarragh Gdns. BT11	21	D12
Owenvarragh Pk.		
Owenvarragh Pk. BT11	20	C11
Oxford St. BT1	16	J8

Street			
Pacific Av. BT15	10	G5
Pakenham St. BT7	16	H9
Palace Gdns. BT15	10	G4
Palace Gro., Hol. BT18	13	P4
Palestine St. BT7	22	H10
Palmer Ct. BT13	9	E6
Palmer St.		
Palmer St. BT13	9	E6
Palmerston Pk. BT4	18	M7
Palmerston Rd. BT4	18	M7
Pandora St. BT12	15	G9 •
Pansy St. BT4	17	L8
Panton St. BT12	15	F8
Ross Rd.		
Paris St. BT13	15	F7
Park Av. BT4	17	L7
Park Av., Hol. BT18	7	Q2
Park Dr., Hol. BT18	7	Q2

Street			
Park Gra. BT4	17	M8
Park Av.		
Park La. BT9	22	G10
Park Par. BT6	16	J9
Park Pl. BT6	17	K9
Park Rd. BT7	23	J11
Parkend St. BT15	10	H5
Parker St.		
Parkgate Av. BT4	17	L8
Parkgate Cres. BT4	17	L8
Parkgate Dr. BT4	17	L8
Parkgate Gdns. BT4	17	L8
Parkgate Par. BT4	17	L8
Parkmore St. BT7	23	J11
Parkmount Clo. BT15	10	H5
Parkmount Gdns. BT15	5	H2
Parkmount La. BT15	5	H2
Parkmount Par. BT15	5	H2
Parkmount Pas. BT15	5	H2
Parkmount Pl. BT15	5	H2
Parkmount Rd. BT15	4	G3
Parkmount St. BT15	10	H6
Parkmount Ter. BT15	5	H2
Parkmount Way BT15	5	H2
Parkside Gdns. BT15	10	H5
Parkview Ct. BT14	10	F6
Glenview St.		
Parkville Ct. BT15	10	G4
Parkway BT4	13	O6
Pasadena Gdns. BT5	18	N9
Pattersons Pl. BT1	16	H8
Upper Arthur St.		
Pattons La., Hol. BT18	7	Q2
Church Vw.		
Paulett Av. BT5	17	K8
Albert Bri. Rd.		
Pavilions Pk., Hol. BT18	7	P2
Paxton St. BT5	17	K9
Pearl St. BT6	17	K9
Pembridge Ct. BT4	18	O8
Pembridge Ms. BT5	18	N9
Pembroke St. BT12	15	F9
Penge Gdns. BT9	22	H12
Penrose St. BT7	22	H10
Percy Pl. BT13	15	G7
Percy St. BT13	15	G8
Pernau St. BT13	15	F7
Perry Ct. BT5	17	K8
Peters Hill BT13	16	G7
Picardy Av. BT6	23	L11
Pilot Pl. BT1	16	J7
Pilot St.		
Pilot St. BT1	16	J7
Pim St. BT15	16	G7
Pims Av. BT4	17	M8
Pine Crest, Hol. BT18	7	Q3
Pine Gro., Hol. BT18	7	P3
Loughview Av.		
Pine St. BT7	16	H9
Pine Way BT7	16	H9
Pinkerton Wk. BT15	10	H6
Pirrie Pk. Gdns. BT6	23	K10
Pirrie Rd. BT4	18	O8
Pitt Pl. BT4	17	K8
Pittsburg St. BT15	10	H5
Plevna Pk. BT12	15	F8
Osman St.		
Plunket Ct. BT13	16	H7
Alton Ct.		
Pollard Clo. BT12	15	E8
Pollard St. BT12	15	E8
Pollock Rd. BT3	11	J6
Pommern Par. BT6	24	L10
Pomona Av. BT4	17	M8
Ponsonby Av. BT15	10	G6
Portallo St. BT6	17	K9
Portland La. BT15	16	H7
Portland St.		
Portland St. BT15	16	H7
Portnamona Ct. BT11	20	C10
Posnett Ct. BT7	16	H9
Posnett St. BT7	16	H9
Pottinger St. BT5	17	K9
Pottingers Ct. BT1	16	H8
Ann St.		
Pottingers Entry BT1	16	H8
High St.		
Powerscourt Pl. BT7	22	H10
Powerscourt St. BT7	22	H10
Premier Dr. BT15	10	H4
Premier Gro. BT15	10	H4
Prestwick Dr. BT14	9	E4
Prestwick Pk. BT14	9	E4
Pretoria St. BT9	22	H11
Primitive St. BT7	15	E9
Donegall Rd.		
Primrose St. BT7	23	J11
Primrose St. BT14	9	E5
Prince Andrew Gdns. BT12	15	G9
Prince Andrew Pk.		
Prince Andrew Pk. BT12	15	G9
Prince Edward Dr. BT9	22	H12
Prince Edward Gdns. BT9	22	H12
Prince Edward Pk. BT9	22	H12
Prince of Wales Av. BT4	19	P8
Prince Regent Rd. BT5	24	M11
Princes Ct. BT1	16	H8
Princes St.		
Princes Dock St. BT1	16	J7
Princes St. BT1	16	H8
Princes St. Ct. BT1	16	H8
Princes St.		
Princess Gdns., Hol. BT18	7	R2
Prior's Lea, Hol. BT18	13	P4
Firmount Cres.		
Priory End, Hol. BT18	7	P3
Priory Gdns. BT10	21	D13

Street	Page	Grid
Priory Pk. BT10	21	D13
Priory Pk., Hol. BT18	7	Q2
Private Av. (Dundonald) BT16	19	R9
Prospect St. BT7	16	H9
Prospect Ter., Hol. BT18	7	P2
Kinnegar Rd.		
Quadrant Pl. BT12	15	G8
Divis Flats		
Quarry Rd. BT4	13	O6
Queen Elizabeth Bri. BT1	16	J8
Queen Elizabeth Bri. BT3	16	J8
Queen St. BT1	16	H8
Queen Victoria Gdns. BT15	10	H4
Queen Victoria St. BT5	17	L8
Queens Aro. BT1	16	H8
Fountain St.		
Queen's Bri. BT1	16	J8
Queen's Bri. BT4	16	J8
Queens Par. BT15	10	H6
Queens Quay BT3	16	J8
Queens Quay Link BT3	16	J8
Bridge End		
Queens Quay Rd. BT3	16	J7
Queens Rd. BT3	16	J7
Queens Sq. BT1	16	H8
Queensberry Pk. BT6	23	K12
Queensland St. BT13	15	F7
Quinns Ct. BT4	17	K8
Newtownards Rd.		
Quinns Pl. BT15	16	H7
Nelson St.		
Quinton St. BT5	17	L9
Quinville, Hol. BT18	7	Q2
Spencer St.		
Raby St. BT7	23	J11
Radnor St. BT6	17	K9
Raglan St. BT12	15	F8
Leeson St.		
Railway St. BT12	16	G9
Rainey Way BT7	16	H9
Lindsay St.		
Raleigh St. BT13	15	F7
Ramoan Dr. BT11	20	B11
Ramoan Gdns. BT11	20	B11
Randal Pk. BT9	22	F12
Ranelagh St. BT6	23	K10
Ranfurly Dr. BT4	18	M8
Raphael St. BT7	16	H9
Ratcliffe St. BT7	16	H9
Rathbone St. BT2	16	H8
Little May St.		
Rathcool St. BT9	22	F11
Rathdrum St. BT9	22	F11
Rathgar St. BT9	22	F11
Rathlin St. BT13	9	E6
Rathmore St. BT6	17	K9
Ravenhill Av. BT6	17	K9
Ravenhill Ct. BT6	23	K10
Ravenhill Cres. BT6	17	K9
Ravenhill Gdns. BT6	23	J10
Ravenhill Par. BT6	23	K10
Ravenhill Pk. BT6	23	J11
Ravenhill Pk. Gdns. BT6	23	K11
Ravenhill Reach BT6	16	J9
Ravenhill Reach Clo. BT6	16	J9
Ravenhill Reach Ct. BT6	16	J9
Ravenhill Reach		
Ravenhill Reach Ms. BT6	16	J9
Ravenhill Rd. BT6	23	J11
Ravenhill St. BT6	17	K9
Ravenscroft Av. BT5	17	L8
Ravenscroft St. BT5	17	L8
Ravensdale Cres. BT5	17	L9
Ravensdale St. BT5	17	L9
Ravensdene Cres. BT6	23	K11
Ravensdene Ms. BT6	23	J10
Ravensdene Pk. BT6	23	J11
Ravensdene Pk. Gdns. BT6	23	K11
Ravenswood Cres. BT5	25	O11
Ravenswood Pk. BT5	25	O11
Redburn Sq., Hol. BT18	7	P2
Redcar St. BT6	17	K9
Redcliffe Dr. BT4	17	L8
Redcliffe Par. BT4	17	L8
Redcliffe St. BT4	17	L8
Regent St. BT13	16	G7
Reid St. BT6	23	K10
Renfrew Ho. BT12	16	G9
Rowland Way		
Renfrew Wk. BT12	16	G9
Rowland Way		
Renwick St. BT12	16	G9
Riada Clo. BT4	17	K8
Ribble St. BT4	17	L8
Richardson Ct. BT6	17	K9
Richardson St.		
Richardson St. BT6	17	K9
Richdale Dr., Hol. BT18	7	R1
Richhill Cres. BT5	18	N9
Richhill Pk. BT5	18	N9
Richmond La. BT15	4	G3
Antrim Rd.		
Richmond Ms. BT10	21	D13
Richmond Pk.		
Richmond Pk. BT9	22	G12
Richmond Pk. BT10	21	D13
Richmond Sq. BT15	10	G5
Richview St. BT12	15	F9
Riddels Arc. BT1	16	H8
Fountain St.		
Ridgeway St. BT9	22	H11
Riga St. BT13	15	F7
Rileys Ct. BT7	16	H9
Rileys Pl. BT7	16	H9
Ringford Cres. BT11	20	A12
Ringford Pk. BT11	20	B12
Ringford Cres.		
Rinnalea Clo. BT11	20	A12
Rinnalea Gdns. BT11	20	A12
Rinnalea Gro. BT11	20	A12
Rinnalea Wk. BT11	20	A12
Rinnalea Way		
Rinnalea Way BT11	20	A12
Ritchie St. BT15	10	H5
River Clo. BT11	20	B12
River Ter. BT7	16	J9
Riverdale Clo. BT11	20	C12
Riverdale Gdns. BT11	20	C12
Riverdale Pk. Av. BT11	20	C12
Riverdale Pk. Dr. BT11	20	C12
Riverdale Pk. E. BT11	20	C12
Riverdale Pk. N. BT11	20	C12
Riverdale Pk. S. BT11	20	C12
Riverdale Pk. W. BT11	20	C12
Riverdale Pl. BT11	20	C12
Riverdale St. BT13	16	G7
North Boundary St.		
Riverdale Ter. BT10	21	D12
Riverside, Hol. BT18	7	Q2
Riverside Sq. BT12	15	F9
Roden Way		
Riverside Way BT12	15	G9
Riverview St. BT9	22	H11
Robina Ct. BT15	10	H6
Robina St. BT15	10	H6
Rochester Av. BT6	24	L11
Rochester Dr. BT6	24	L11
Rochester Rd. BT6	24	L12
Rochester St. BT6	17	K9
Rock Gro. BT12	14	D9
Glenalina Cres.		
Rockdale St. BT12	15	E9
Rockland St. BT12	15	F9
Rockmore Rd. BT12	15	E9
Rockmount St. BT12	15	E9
Rockview St. BT12	21	F10
Rockville St. BT12	15	E9
Rocky Rd. BT5	25	P11
Rocky Rd. BT8	24	L12
Roddens Cres. BT5	24	N11
Roddens Gdns. BT5	24	N11
Roddens Pk. BT5	24	N11
Roden Ct. BT12	15	F9
Roden St.		
Roden Pas. BT12	15	F9
Roden Sq. BT12	15	F9
Roden Way		
Roden St. BT12	15	F9
Roden Way BT12	15	F9
Rodney Dr. BT12	21	E10
Rodney Par. BT12	21	E10
Roe St. BT14	10	G6
Roosevelt Ri. BT12	15	F9
Roosevelt St.		
Roosevelt Sq. BT12	15	F9
Roosevelt St.		
Roosevelt St. BT12	15	F9
Rosapenna Ct. BT14	10	G6
Rosapenna St.		
Rosapenna Dr. BT14	10	G6
Rosapenna Par. BT14	10	G6
Rosapenna Sq. BT11	20	A12
Rosapenna St. BT14	10	G6
Rosapenna Wk. BT14	10	G6
Rosevale St.		
Rosebank Ct. BT14	10	F6
Glenview St.		
Rosebank St. BT13	9	F6
Ohio St.		
Rosebery Gdns. BT6	17	K9
Rosebery Rd. BT6	17	K9
Rosebery St. BT5	17	L8
Roseland Pl. BT12	15	E9
Donegall Rd.		
Roseleigh St. BT14	10	G6
Rosemary St. BT1	16	H8
Rosemount Av. BT5	19	Q9
Rosemount Gdns. BT15	10	G5
Rosemount Pk. BT5	24	N12
Rosepark BT5	19	Q9
Rosepark Cen. BT5	19	Q9
Rosepark E. BT5	19	Q9
Rosepark Meadows BT5	19	Q9
Rosepark		
Rosepark S. BT5	19	Q9
Rosepark W. BT5	19	Q9
Rosetta Av. BT7	23	J12
Rosetta Dr. BT7	23	J12
Rosetta Par. BT7	23	J12
Rosetta Pk. BT6	23	J12
Rosetta Rd. BT6	23	K12
Rosetta Rd. E. BT6	23	K12
Rosetta Way BT6	23	J12
Rosevale Pk. BT5	18	O9
Rosevale St. BT14	10	G6
Rosewood Ct. BT14	10	F6
Rosewood St.		
Rosewood Pk. BT6	24	N11
Rosewood St. BT14	10	F6
Rosgoill Dr. BT11	20	B12
Rosgoill Gdns. BT11	20	B12
Rosgoill Pk. BT11	20	B11
Roslin Gdns. BT5	19	Q9
Roslyn St. BT6	17	K9
Ross Cotts. BT12	15	G8
Ross Rd.		
Ross St. BT12	15	F8
Ross Ri. BT12	15	F8
Ross Rd.		
Ross Rd. BT12	15	F8
Ross St. BT12	15	G8
Rosscoole Pk. BT14	4	F3
Rossmore Av. BT7	23	J11
Rossmore Cres. BT7	23	J12
Rossmore Dr. BT7	23	J12
Rossmore Pk. BT7	23	J12
Rossnareen Av. BT11	20	B11
Rossnareen Ct. BT11	20	B11
Rossnareen Pk. BT11	20	B11
Rossnareen Rd. BT11	20	B11
Rothsay Sq. BT14	10	F6
Rothsay St. BT14	10	F6
Glenpark St.		
Rotterdam Ct. BT5	16	J8
Rotterdam St. BT5	16	J8
Roumania Ri. BT12	15	G8
Roundhill St. BT5	17	K8
Rowland Way BT12	16	G9
Royal Av. BT1	16	H8
Rugby Av. BT7	22	H10
Rugby Ct. BT7	22	H10
Rugby Ms. BT7	22	H10
Rugby St.		
Rugby Par. BT7	22	H10
Rugby Rd. BT7	22	H10
Rugby St. BT7	22	H10
Rumford St. BT13	15	G7
Runnymede Dr. BT12	22	F10
Runnymede Par. BT12	22	F10
Rushfield Av. BT7	23	J11
Rusholme St. BT13	15	F7
Snugville St.		
Russell Pk. BT5	25	Q10
Russell Pl. BT2	16	H9
Joy St.		
Russell St. BT2	16	H9
Ruth St. BT15	10	H6
Rutherford St. BT13	15	G7
Hopewell Cres.		
Rutherglen St. BT13	9	E6
Rutland St. BT7	23	J10
Ryan Pk. BT5	24	N13
Rydalmere St. BT12	15	F9
Sackville Ct. BT13	15	G8
Sagimore Gdns. BT5	17	M9
St. Agnes Dr. BT11	20	C11
St. Agnes Pl. BT11	20	C11
St. Albans Gdns. BT9	22	G11
St. Andrews Sq. E. BT12	16	G9
Hope St.		
St. Andrews Sq. N. BT12	16	G9
Hope St.		
St. Andrews Sq. W. BT12	16	G9
Hope St.		
St. Aubyn St. BT15	11	J5
St. Columbans St. BT14	10	F6
Glenview St.		
St. Gemmas St. BT14	10	F6
St. Georges Gdns. BT12	16	G9
Albion St.		
St. Helens Ct., Hol. BT18	7	P2
St. Ives Gdns. BT9	22	G11
St. James Av. BT14	14	D7
Highcairn Dr.		
St. James's Av. BT12	15	E9
St. James's Cres. BT12	21	E10
St. James's Dr. BT12	15	E9
St. James's Gdns. BT12	15	E9
St. James's Par. BT12	15	E9
St. James's Pk. BT12	15	E9
St. James's Pl. BT12	15	E9
St. James's St. BT14	10	G6
St. Johns Av. BT7	23	J12
St. Johns Ct. BT7	23	J12
St. Johns Pk.		
St. Johns Pk. BT7	23	J12
St. Judes Av. BT7	23	J11
St. Judes Cres. BT7	23	J11
St. Judes Dr. BT7	16	H9
Ormeau Rd.		
St. Judes Par. BT7	23	J11
St. Judes Path BT12	16	G8
Cullingtree Rd.		
St. Judes Row BT12	16	G8
Cullingtree Rd.		
St. Judes Wk. BT12	16	G8
Cullingtree Rd.		
St. Katharine Rd. BT12	21	E10
St. Kilda Ct. BT6	16	J9
St. Kilda St. BT6	16	J9
St. Leonard's Cres. BT4	17	K8
St. Leonards St.		
St. Leonards St. BT4	17	K8
St. Lukes Clo. BT13	15	G7
Carlow St.		
St. Lukes Wk. BT13	15	G7
Percy St.		
St. Marys Ct. BT13	15	F7
Silvio St.		
St. Matthew's Ct. BT5	17	K8
Seaforde St.		
St. Meryl Pk. BT11	20	C10
St. Patricks Wk. BT4	17	K8
Newtownards Rd.		
St. Pauls Fold BT15	10	H6
St. Pauls St. BT15	10	H6
Canning St.		
St. Peters Ct. BT12	15	G8
St. Peter's Pl. BT12	15	G8
Divis Flats		
St. Peters Sq. E. BT12	15	G8
Divis Flats		

Name	Page	Grid
St. Peters Sq. N. BT12	15	G8
Divis Flats		
St. Peters Sq. S. BT12	15	G8
Divis Flats		
St. Stephens Ct. BT13	16	G7
Brown Sq.		
St. Vincent St. BT15	11	J5
Saintfield Rd. BT8	23	J13
Saleen Pk., Hol. BT18	7	Q2
Priory Pk.		
Salisbury Av. BT15	10	G4
Salisbury Ct. BT7	16	H9
Salisbury Gdns. BT15	4	G3
Salisbury La. BT7	16	H9
Salisbury St.		
Salisbury St. BT7	16	H9
Samuel St. BT1	16	H7
Sancroft St. BT13	15	F7
Sandbrook Gdns. BT4	17	M7
Sandbrook Gro. BT4	17	M7
Sandbrook Pk. BT4	17	M7
Sandford Av. BT5	18	M9
Sandhill Dr. BT5	18	M9
Sandhill Gdns. BT5	18	N9
Sandhill Grn. BT5	18	N9
Sandhill Par. BT5	18	N9
Sandhill Pk. BT5	18	M9
Sandhurst Ct. BT9	22	H11
Colenso Par.		
Sandhurst Dr. BT9	22	H11
Sandhurst Gdns. BT9	22	H11
Sandhurst Rd. BT7	22	H10
Sandown Dr. BT5	18	N9
Sandown Pk. BT5	18	N9
Sandown Pk. S. BT5	18	N9
Sandown Rd. BT5	18	N9
Sandringham Ms. BT5	18	O9
Sandringham St. BT9	22	G10
Sandy Row BT12	16	G9
Sandymount St. BT9	22	G11
Sans Souci Pk. BT9	22	G11
Santiago St. BT13	15	F7
Madras St.		
Sarajac Cres. BT14	4	F3
Sark St. BT4	17	K8
Newcastle St.		
Saul St. BT5	17	K8
Vulcan St.		
Saunders Clo. BT4	17	K8
Saunderson Ct. BT14	10	F6
Glenpark St.		
Sawel Hill BT11	20	C11
Schomberg Av. BT4	18	O7
Schomberg Dr. BT12	16	G9
Aughrim Pk.		
Schomberg Pk. BT4	18	O7
School Ct. BT4	13	O5
Scotch Row BT4	17	K8
Newtownards Rd.		
Scott St. BT12	16	G9
Scrabo St. BT5	16	J8
Station St.		
Seabank Par. BT15	10	H4
Seabourne Par. BT15	10	H4
Seaforde Ct. BT5	17	K8
Seaforde St.		
Seaforde Gdns. BT5	17	K8
Seaforde St.		
Seaforde St. BT5	17	K8
Seagrove Par. BT15	10	H4
Seagrove Pl. BT15	10	H4
Premier Dr.		
Seaholm Par. BT15	10	H4
Seal Rd. BT3	11	K5
Sealands Par. BT15	10	H4
Seamount St. BT15	10	H4
Seamount Par. BT15	10	H4
Seapark Av., Hol. BT18	7	Q1
Seapark Ct. BT15	10	H4
Seapark Dr. BT15	10	H4
Seapark Rd., Hol. BT18	7	Q1
Seapark Ter., Hol. BT18	7	Q1
Seascape Par. BT15	10	H4
Seaview Clo. BT15	10	H5
Seaview Dr. BT15	10	H4
Seaview Gdns. BT15	10	H4
Seaview St. BT15	10	H5
Seaview Ter., Hol. BT18	7	Q2
Birch Dr.		
Sefton Dr. BT4	17	M8
Sefton Pk. BT4	17	M8
Selby Ct. BT12	15	F9
Selby Wk. BT12	15	F9
Selby Ct.		
Selkirk Row BT5	19	Q9
Granton Pk.		
Servia St. BT12	15	G8
Sevastopol St. BT13	15	F8
Severn St. BT4	17	L8
Seymour La. BT1	16	H8
Seymour St.		
Seymour Row BT1	16	H8
Seymour St. BT1	16	H8
Seymour St. BT2	16	H8
Shaftesbury Arc. BT2	16	H9
Dublin Rd.		
Shaftesbury Sq. BT7	16	J9
Shaftesbury Sq. BT2	16	H9
Shalom Pk. BT6	24	N11
Shamrock Ct. BT6	17	K9
Mount St. S.		
Shamrock Pl. BT6	17	K9
Shamrock St. BT6	17	K9
Shancoole Pk. BT14	4	F3
Shandarragh Pk. BT15	4	G3
Shandon Ct. BT5	24	N11
Shandon Pk. BT5	25	O10
Shaneen Pk. BT14	4	F3
Shangarry Pk. BT14	4	F3
Shankill Par. BT13	16	G7
Shankill Rd. BT13	15	F7
Shankill Ter. BT13	16	G7
North Boundary St.		
Shanlieve Pk. BT14	4	F3
Shanlieve Rd. BT11	20	C11
Leeson St.		
Shannon Ct. BT14	10	G6
Shannon St. BT14	10	G6
Sharman Clo. BT9	22	H12
Sharman Dr. BT9	22	H12
Sharman Gdns. BT9	22	H12
Sharman Pk. BT9	22	H12
Sharman Rd. BT9	22	H12
Sharman Way BT9	22	H12
Shaw St. BT4	17	M8
Shaws Av. BT11	20	B11
Shaws Clo. BT11	20	B11
Shaws Ct. BT11	20	B11
Shaws Pk. BT11	20	B11
Shaws Pl. BT11	20	B11
Shaws Rd. BT11	20	B11
Shelbourne Rd. BT6	23	K10
Sherbrook Clo. BT13	16	G7
Sherbrook Ter. BT13	16	G7
Denmark St.		
Sheridan Ct. BT13	10	H6
Sheridan St.		
Sheridan St. BT15	10	H6
Sheriff St. BT5	17	K8
Vulcan St.		
Sheringhurst Pk. BT15	5	H3
Sherloan St. BT15	10	H6
Sherwood St. BT6	17	K9
Sheskin Way BT6	23	K11
Shiels St. BT12	15	E9
Shimna Clo. BT6	23	K11
Ship St. BT15	11	J6
Shipbuoy St. BT15	16	H7
Shore Cres. BT15	5	J2
Shore Rd. BT15	10	H4
Shore St., Hol. BT18	7	Q2
Short Strand BT5	16	J8
Short St. BT1	16	J7
Shrewsbury Dr. BT9	21	F13
Shrewsbury Gdns. BT9	21	E13
Shrewsbury Pk. BT9	21	F13
Sicily Pk. BT10	21	D13
Silver Birch Cts. BT18	15	F7
Silverstream Av. BT14	9	E4
Silverstream Cres. BT14	9	D4
Silverstream Dr. BT14	9	E4
Silverstream Gdns. BT14	9	E4
Silverstream Par. BT14	9	E4
Silverstream Pk. BT14	9	E4
Silverstream Rd. BT14	9	D4
Silverstream Ter. BT14	9	D4
Silvio St. BT13	15	F7
Simpsons Ct. BT7	16	H9
Ormeau Rd.		
Sinclair Rd. BT3	11	K5
Sinclair St. BT5	18	N9
Sintonville Av. BT5	17	M8
Siulnamona Ct. BT11	20	C10
Aitnamona Cres.		
Skegoneill Av. BT15	10	G4
Skegoneill Dr. BT15	10	H5
Skegoneill St. BT15	11	J5
Skipper St. BT1	16	H8
Skipton St. BT5	17	L8
Slate St. BT12	15	F8
Grosvenor Rd.		
Slemish Way BT11	20	C11
Slieveban Dr. BT11	20	C11
Slievecoole Pk. BT14	4	F3
Slievedarragh Pk. BT14	4	F3
Slievegallion Dr. BT11	20	C11
Slievemoyne Pk. BT15	4	G3
Slievetoye Pk. BT14	4	F3
Sloan Ct. BT9	22	F10
Smithfield BT1	16	H8
Francis St.		
Smithfield Mkt. BT1	16	H8
Francis St.		
Snugville St. BT13	15	F7
Solway St. BT4	17	K8
Somerdale Gdns. BT14	9	E6
Somerdale Pk. BT14	9	E6
Somerset St. BT7	23	J11
Somerton Clo. BT15	10	G4
Somerton Dr. BT15	10	H4
Somerton Gdns. BT15	10	H4
Somerton Gra. BT15	5	H3
Somerton Pk. BT15	5	H3
Somerton Rd. BT15	10	H4
Somme Dr. BT6	23	L11
Sorella St. BT12	15	F8
Soudan St. BT12	22	F10
South Av. BT15	10	G4
South Bk. BT6	23	K11
South Clo., Hol. BT18	7	P3
South Grn. BT11	20	C11
South Link BT11	20	C11
South Par. BT7	23	J11
South Sperrin BT5	19	Q9
Southland Dale BT5	25	O11
Southport Ct. BT14	10	G6
Mountview St.		
Southview Cotts. BT7	22	H11
Stranmillis Embk.		
Southview St. BT7	22	H10
Southwell St. BT13	16	G8
Brown St.		
Southwell St. BT15	16	H7
Spamount St. BT15	10	H6
Spencer Rd. BT3	11	J6
Spencer St., Hol. BT18	7	Q2
Sperrin Dr. BT5	19	Q9
Sperrin Pk. BT5	19	Q9
Spiers Pl. BT13	15	F7
Spinner Sq. BT12	15	F8
Leeson St.		
Spinner St. BT12	15	F8
Spinnershill La. BT14	9	D4
Old Mill Rd.		
Spires, The, Hol. BT18	7	R3
Spring Pl. BT6	17	K9
Spring St.		
Spring St. BT6	17	K9
Springdale Gdns. BT13	15	E8
Springfield Av. BT12	15	E8
Springfield Clo. BT13	14	D8
Springfield Ct. BT12	15	F8
Springfield Cres. BT12	15	E8
Springfield Dr. BT12	15	E8
Springfield Heights BT13	14	D8
Springfield Par. BT13	14	D8
Springfield Pk. BT13	14	D8
Springfield Rd. BT12	14	C8
Springhill Av. BT12	14	D8
Springhill Clo. BT12	14	D8
Springhill Cres. BT12	14	D8
Springhill Dr. BT12	14	D9
Springhill Gdns. BT12	14	D8
Springhill Heights BT12	14	D8
Springhill Ri. BT12	14	D9
Springmadden Ct. BT12	14	D8
Springhill Cres.		
Springmartin Rd. BT13	14	D8
Springvale Dr. BT14	9	D4
Springvale Gdns. BT14	9	D4
Springvale Par. BT14	9	D4
Springvale Pk. BT14	9	D4
Springview St. BT13	15	F8
Springview Wk. BT13	15	F8
Malcolmson St.		
Squires Hill Cres. BT14	9	D4
Squires Hill Pk. BT14	9	D4
Squires Hill Rd. BT14	9	D4
Stable La. BT1	16	H8
Wellington St.		
Stanfield Pl. BT7	16	J9
Stanfield Row BT7	16	J9
Lower Stanfield St.		
Stanhope Dr. BT13	16	G7
Stanley Ct. BT12	16	G8
Albert St.		
Stanley La. BT15	16	H7
Little York St.		
Stanley Pl. BT15	16	H7
Little York St.		
Stanley St. BT12	16	G8
Station Ms. (Sydenham) BT4	18	N7
Station Rd. BT4	18	M7
Station Rd., Hol. BT18	7	R1
Station St. BT3	16	J8
Station St. Flyover BT3	16	J8
Steam Mill La. BT1	16	J7
Steens Back Row BT5	17	L9
Abetta Par.		
Steens Row BT5	17	L9
Stephen St. BT1	16	H7
Stewart St. BT7	16	J9
Stewarts Pl., Hol. BT18	7	Q2
Strand Av.		
Stewartstown Av. BT11	20	A11
Stewartstown Gdns. BT11	20	B12
Stewartstown Pk. BT11	20	A11
Stewartstown Rd. BT11	20	A13
Stewartstown Rd. (Dunmurry) BT17	20	A13
Stirling Av. BT6	24	L11
Stirling Gdns. BT6	24	L11
Stirling Rd. BT6	24	L11
Stockmans Av. BT11	21	D11
Stockmans Ct. BT11	21	D11
Stockmans Cres. BT11	21	D11
Stockmans Dr. BT11	21	D11
Stockmans Av.		
Stockmans Gdns. BT11	21	D11
Stockmans Av.		
Stockmans La. BT9	21	D12
Stockmans La. BT11	21	D11
Stockmans Pk. BT11	21	D11
Stockmans Way BT9	21	D12
Stoney Rd. BT4	19	Q8
Stoney Rd. (Dundonald) BT16	19	Q8
Stoneycairn Ct. BT14	8	C4
Mountainhill Rd.		
Stonyford St. BT5	17	L8
Stormont Castle BT4	19	Q7
Stormont Ct. BT4	19	P9
Stormont Pk. BT4	19	P8
Stormont Rd. BT3	11	K5
Stormont Vills. BT4	19	P7
Stormont Cres. BT5	17	K9
Stormont St.		
Stormont La. BT5	17	K9
Stormont St. BT5	17	K9
Stornoway Row BT5	19	Q9
Granton Pk.		
Stracam Cor. BT6	23	L12
Straight, The BT6	23	K12
Strand, The, Hol. BT18	7	Q2
Strand Av., Hol. BT18	7	Q2
Strand Clo. BT5	17	K8
Vulcan St.		
Strand Ct. BT5	17	L9
Avoniel Rd.		

Street	Map	Grid
Strand Ms. BT5	17	K8
Strand Ms., Hol. BT18	7	Q2
Strand Wk. BT5	17	K8
Vulcan St.		
Strandburn Ct. BT4	17	M7
Strandburn Gdns.		
Strandburn Cres. BT4	18	M7
Strandburn Dr. BT4	18	M7
Strandburn Gdns. BT4	17	M7
Strandburn Par. BT4	18	M7
Strandburn Pk. BT4	18	M7
Strandburn St. BT4	17	M7
Strandview St. BT9	22	H11
Strangford Av. BT9	21	E13
Stranmillis Ct. BT9	22	H11
Stranmillis Embk. BT7	22	H11
Stranmillis Embk. BT9	22	H11
Stranmillis Gdns. BT9	22	H11
Stranmillis Ms. BT9	22	H11
Stranmillis Pk. BT9	22	H11
Stranmillis Rd. BT9	22	G10
Stranmillis St. BT9	22	H11
Stratford Gdns. BT14	9	E5
Strathearn Ct., Hol. BT18	7	P3
Strathearn Ms. BT4	18	N8
Strathearn Pk. BT4	18	O7
Stratheden St. BT15	10	H6
Strathmore Pk. BT15	4	G3
Strathmore Pk. N. BT15	4	G3
Strathmore Pk. S. BT15	4	G3
Strathroy Pk. BT14	9	E6
Stroud St. BT12	16	G9
Sturgeon St. BT12	16	G9
Linfield Rd.		
Suffolk Av. BT11	20	B12
Suffolk Cres. BT11	20	B12
Suffolk Dr. BT11	20	B12
Suffolk Par. BT11	20	B12
Suffolk Rd. BT11	20	A12
Sugarfield St. BT13	15	F8
Sugarhouse Entry BT1	16	H8
Waring St.		
Sullivan Clo., Hol. BT18	7	P2
Sullivan Pl., Hol. BT18	7	P2
Sullivan St., Hol. BT18	7	Q2
Sultan Sq. BT12	15	G8
Servia St.		
Sultan Way BT12	15	G8
Osman St.		
Summer St. BT14	10	G6
Summerhill Av. BT5	19	Q9
Summerhill Ct. BT14	10	G6
Summerhill Dr. BT5	19	P9
Summerhill Pk.		
Summerhill Par. BT5	19	P9
Summerhill Pk. BT5	19	P9
Sunbury Av. BT5	18	M9
Sunderland Rd. BT6	24	L11
Sunningdale Dr. BT14	4	F3
Sunningdale Gdns. BT14	4	F4
Sunningdale Grn. BT14	4	F3
Sunningdale Gro. BT14	4	F4
Sunningdale Pk. BT14	4	F4
Sunningdale Pk. N. BT14	4	F3
Sunninghill Dr. BT14	4	F4
Sunninghill Gdns. BT14	4	F4
Sunninghill Pk. BT14	4	F4
Sunnyside Cres. BT7	22	H11
Sunnyside Dr. BT7	23	J11
Sunnyside Pk. BT7	22	H11
Sunnyside St. BT7	22	H11
Sunwich St. BT6	23	K10
Surrey St. BT9	22	F11
Susan St. BT5	17	K8
Sussex Pl. BT2	16	H8
Swift Pl. BT6	17	K9
Swift St.		
Swift St. BT6	17	K9
Sycamore Gro. BT4	18	M7
Sydenham Av. BT4	18	N8
Sydenham Bypass BT3	17	L7
Sydenham Cres. BT4	18	M7
Sydenham Dr. BT4	18	M8
Sydenham Gdns. BT4	18	M7
Sydenham Pk. BT4	18	M7
Sydenham Rd. BT3	16	J7
Sydney St. W. BT13	15	F7
Sylvan St. BT14	10	G6
Symons St. BT12	15	F9
Syringa St. BT15	10	H6
Upper Mervue St.		
Talbot St. BT1	16	H7
Tamar Ct. BT4	17	L8
Tamar St.		
Tamar St. BT4	17	L8
Tamery Pas. BT6	17	K9
Willowfield St.		
Tamery St. BT6	17	K9
Tarawood Ms. BT8	23	J13
Tardree Pk. BT11	20	C11
Tasmania St. BT13	15	F7
Tates Av. BT9	22	F10
Tates Av. BT12	22	F10
Tates Ms. BT9	22	G10
Tates Row, New. BT36	5	J2
Shore Rd.		
Taunton Av. BT15	5	H3
Tavanagh St. BT12	21	F10
Taylor St. BT12	16	H9
Norwood St.		
Tedburn Pk. BT14	9	D5
Telfair St. BT1	16	H8
Temple St. BT5	17	L9
Templemore Av. BT5	17	K8
Templemore Clo. BT5	17	L8
Beersbridge Rd.		
Templemore Pl. BT5	17	L8
Beersbridge Rd.		
Templemore St. BT5	17	L8
Tennent St. BT13	15	F7
Tern St. BT4	17	L8
Teutonic Gdns. BT12	16	G9
Thalia St. BT12	15	G9
Thames Ct. BT12	15	F9
Thames St. BT12	15	F9
Theodore St. BT12	15	F8
Grosvenor Rd.		
Thiepval Av. BT6	23	L11
Third St. BT13	15	F8
Thirlmere Gdns. BT15	4	G3
Thistle Ct. BT5	17	K8
Thomas St. BT15	16	H7
Thompson Pl. BT5	16	J8
Thompson St.		
Thompson St. BT5	16	J8
Thompson Wf. Rd. BT3	11	K6
Thorn St. BT12	16	G9
Blythe St.		
Thorndale Av. BT14	10	G6
Thorndyke St. BT5	17	K8
Thornhill Cres. BT15	19	P9
Thornhill Dr. BT5	19	P9
Thornhill Gdns. BT9	22	F12
Marlborough Pk. S.		
Thornhill Gro. BT5	19	P9
Thornhill Malone BT9	22	F12
Thornhill Par. BT5	19	P9
Thornhill Pk. BT5	19	P9
Tierney Gdns. BT12	16	G9
Tildarg Av. BT11	20	A13
Tildarg St. BT6	23	K10
Tillysburn Dr. BT4	13	O6
Tillysburn Pk.		
Tillysburn Gro. BT4	13	O6
Tillysburn Pk. BT4	13	O6
Timbey Pk. BT7	22	H11
Titania St. BT6	23	K10
Tivoli Gdns. BT15	10	G4
Tobergill St. BT13	15	F7
Tokio Gdns. BT15	10	G4
Tollnamona Ct. BT11	20	C10
Aitnamona Cres.		
Tomb St. BT1	16	H7
Toronto St. BT6	17	K9
Torrens Av. BT14	10	F5
Torrens Ct. BT14	10	F5
Torrens Rd.		
Torrens Cres. BT14	10	F5
Torrens Dr. BT14	10	F5
Torrens Gdns. BT14	10	F5
Torrens Par. BT14	10	F5
Torrens Rd. BT14	10	F5
Tower Ct. BT5	17	K8
Susan St.		
Tower St. BT5	17	K8
Townsend St. BT13	16	G8
Townsley St. BT4	17	K8
Newtownards Rd.		
Trafalgar St. BT15	16	J7
Trainfield St. BT15	10	H6
Tralee St. BT13	15	F8
Tramway St. BT15	10	H6
Lilliput St.		
Trassey Clo. BT6	23	K11
Trench Av. BT11	20	C12
Trench Pk. BT11	20	C12
Trenchard BT11	20	B13
Trevor St., Hol. BT18	7	Q2
Trigo Par. BT6	24	L10
Trillick Ct. BT5	17	K9
Trillick St.		
Trillick St. BT5	17	K9
Trinity St. BT13	16	H7
Trostan Gdns. BT11	21	D11
Trostan Way BT11	21	D11
Tudor Av. BT6	23	L12
Tudor Dale BT4	18	N7
Tudor Dr. BT6	24	L11
Tudor Oaks, Hol. BT18	7	Q2
Tudor Pl. BT13	15	G7
Tullagh Pk. BT11	20	B11
Tullyard Way BT6	24	M11
Tullymore Dr. BT11	20	B11
Tullymore Gdns. BT11	20	B11
Tullymore Wk. BT11	20	B11
Turin St. BT12	15	G9
Twaddell Av. BT13	9	E6
Tweskard Lo. BT4	19	P7
Tweskard Pk. BT4	19	P7
Twiselside, Hol. BT18	7	Q2
Tyndale Cres. BT14	4	E3
Tyndale Dr. BT14	4	E3
Tyndale Gdns. BT14	9	E4
Tyndale Grn. BT14	4	E3
Tyndale Gro. BT14	4	E3
Tyne St. BT13	15	G7
Tyrone St. BT13	16	H7
Ulster St. BT1	16	H8
Ulsterdale St. BT5	17	L8
Ulsterville Av. BT9	22	F10
Ulsterville Dr. BT9	22	G10
Ulsterville Gdns. BT9	22	F10
Ulsterville Pl. BT9	22	G10
Belgravia Av.		
Union Pl. BT15	16	H7
Great Georges St.		
Union St. BT1	16	H7
Uniondale St. BT5	17	L8
Unity Wk. BT13	16	H7
Alton Ct.		
University Av. BT7	22	H10
University Rd. BT7	22	G10
University Sq. BT7	22	H10
University Sq. Ms. BT7	22	H10
University St. BT7	22	H10
University Ter. BT7	22	G10
University Rd.		
Upper Arthur St. BT1	16	H8
Upper Braniel Rd. BT5	24	N12
Upper Canning St. BT15	10	H6
Upper Castle Pk. BT15	4	F3
Upper Cavehill La. BT14	4	E2
Upper Cavehill Rd. BT15	4	F3
Upper Charleville St. BT13	15	F7
Upper Ch. La. BT1	16	H8
Ann St.		
Upper Clara Cres. BT5	17	L9
Clara Av.		
Upper Cres. BT7	22	H10
Upper Cres. La. BT7	22	H10
Mount Charles		
Upper Frank St. BT5	17	K9
Upper Galwally BT8	23	K13
Upper Galwally Pk. BT8	23	K13
Saintfield Rd.		
Upper Glenfarne St. BT13	15	F7
Upper Kent St. BT1	16	H7
Upper Knockbreda Rd. BT6	23	K13
Upper Knockbreda Rd. BT8	23	K13
Upper Lisburn Rd. BT10	21	D13
Upper Meadow St. BT15	10	H6
Upper Meenan St. BT13	15	F7
Upper Mervue St. BT15	10	H6
Upper Newtownards Rd. BT4	17	M8
Upper Newtownards Rd. (Dundonald) BT16	17	M8
Upper Quarry Rd. BT4	13	P6
Upper Queen St. BT1	16	H8
Upper Riga St. BT13	15	F7
Upper Springfield Rd. BT12	20	A10
Upper Springfield Rd. (Hannahstown) BT17	20	A10
Upper Stanfield St. BT7	16	J9
Lower Stanfield St.		
Upper Townsend Ter. BT13	16	G7
Upperlands Wk. BT5	19	Q9
Abbey Pk.		
Upton Cotts. BT11	21	D10
Upton Ct. BT11	21	D10
Utility St. BT12	15	G9
Utility Wk. BT12	15	G9
Valleyside Clo. BT12	15	E7
Vancouver Dr. BT15	10	G4
Vandyck Cres., New. BT36	5	H1
Vara Dr. BT13	15	E7
Vauxhall Pk. BT9	22	H12
Velsheda Ct. BT14	9	E5
Velsheda Pk. BT14	9	E5
Velsheda Way BT14	9	E5
Ventry La. BT2	16	H9
Ventry St. BT2	16	H9
Vere Foster Wk. BT12	14	C8
Moyard Cres.		
Verner St. BT7	16	J8
Vernon Ct. BT7	16	H9
Vernon St.		
Vernon St. BT7	16	H9
Vicarage St. BT5	17	K8
Vicinage Pk. BT14	10	G6
Vicinage Pl. BT14	10	G6
Vicinage Pk.		
Victor Pl. BT6	17	K9
Victoria Av. BT4	18	M7
Victoria Ct. BT4	18	N7
Victoria Dr. BT4	18	M7
Victoria Gdns. BT15	10	G4
Victoria Par. BT15	16	H7
Victoria Rd. BT3	11	K6
Victoria Rd. BT4	18	M7
Victoria Rd., Hol. BT18	7	Q2
Victoria Sq. BT1	16	H8
Victoria St. BT1	16	H8
Vidor Ct. BT4	18	M7
Victoria Dr.		
Vidor Gdns. BT4	18	M7
Village Grn., The BT6	23	L10
Violet St. BT12	15	F8
Vionville Clo. BT5	19	Q10
Vionville Ct. BT5	19	Q10
Vionville Ri.		
Vionville Grn. BT5	19	Q10
Vionville Ri.		
Vionville Heights BT5	19	Q10
Vionville Ri.		
Vionville Pk. BT5	19	Q10
Vionville Ri.		
Vionville Pl. BT5	19	Q10
Vionville Ri. BT5	19	Q10
Vionville Vw. BT5	19	Q10
Vionville Way BT5	19	Q10
Vionville Ri.		
Virginia St. BT7	16	H9
Virginia Way BT7	16	H9
Vistula St. BT13	10	F6
Vulcan Ct. BT5	17	K8
Vulcan St.		
Vulcan Gdns. BT5	17	K8
Seaforde St.		

Street	Map	Grid
Vulcan Link BT5	17	K8
Vulcan St.		
Vulcan St. BT5	17	K8
Walbeck St. BT15	10	H6
Dawson St.		
Walkers La. BT1	16	H7
Frederick St.		
Wall St. BT13	16	G7
Wallasey Pk. BT14	9	E4
Walmer St. BT7	23	J11
Walnut Ct. BT7	16	H9
Walnut St.		
Walnut Ms. BT7	16	H9
Walnut St. BT7	16	H9
Wandsworth Ct. BT4	18	O8
Wandsworth Cres. BT4	18	O8
Wandsworth Dr. BT4	18	N8
Wandsworth Gdns. BT4	18	N8
Wandsworth Par. BT4	18	N8
Wandsworth Pl. BT4	18	N8
Campbell Pk. Av.		
Wandsworth Rd. BT4	18	N8
Wansbeck St. BT9	22	H12
Ward St. BT12	15	F8
Warehouse La. BT1	16	H8
Waring St.		
Waring St. BT1	16	H8
Warren Gro. BT5	25	O11
Waterford Gdns. BT13	15	F8
Waterford St. BT13	15	F8
Waterford Way BT13	15	F8
Waterford St.		
Waterloo Gdns. BT15	4	G2
Waterloo Pk. BT15	4	G2
Waterloo Pk. N. BT15	4	G2
Waterloo Pk. S. BT15	4	G2
Watermount Cres. BT12	15	E8
Watermouth St. BT12	15	E8
Clovelly St.		
Waterville St. BT13	15	F8
Watkins Rd. BT3	11	J6
Watson St. BT12	16	G9
Watt St. BT6	23	K10
Wauchope Ct. BT12	15	F9
Connaught St.		
Waveney Av. BT15	5	H3
Waveney Dr. BT15	5	H3
Waveney Gro. BT15	5	H3
Waveney Heights BT15	5	H3
Waveney Pk. BT15	5	H3
Wayland St. BT5	17	L9
Wayside Clo. BT5	25	O11
Weavers Ct. BT12	16	G9
Weavershill La. BT14	9	D4
Weavershill Wk. BT14	8	C4
Mountainhill Rd.		
Weir St. BT13	15	F7
Well Pl. BT6	17	K9
Spring St.		
Welland St. BT4	17	L8
Wellesley Av. BT9	22	G10
Wellington Ct. BT1	16	H8
Wellington St.		
Wellington Pk. BT9	22	G10
Wellington Pk. Av. BT9	22	G10
Wellington Pk. Ter. BT9	22	G10
Wellington Pl. BT1	16	H8
Wellington St. BT1	16	H8
Wellwood Av. BT4	17	M7
Wellwood Clo. BT4	17	M7
Wellwood Av.		
Wellwood St. BT12	16	G9
Welsh St. BT7	16	J9
Wesley Ct. BT12	15	E9
Donegall Rd.		
Wesley St. BT12	16	G9
Stroud St.		
West Bk. Clo. BT3	11	L4
West Bk. Dr. BT3	11	L4
West Bk. Rd. BT3	11	L4
West Bk. Way BT3	12	L3
West Circular Cres. BT13	14	D7
West Circular Rd. BT13	14	D8
West Grn., Hol. BT18	7	P3
West Link, Hol. BT18	7	P3
West St. BT1	16	H8
Westbank Rd. BT3	6	N3
Westbourne St. BT5	17	K8
Beechfield St.		
Westcliff Dr. BT12	14	D9
Whiterock Rd.		
Westcott St. BT5	17	L8
Bloomfield Av.		
Westhill Way BT12	14	D9
Glenalina Cres.		
Westland Dr. BT14	4	F4
Westland Gdns. BT14	4	F4
Westland Rd. BT14	10	F5
Westland Way BT14	10	G4
Westlink BT13	16	G7
Westminster Av. BT4	17	L8
Westminster Av. N. BT4	17	L8
Westminster Av.		
Westminster St. BT7	22	H10
Weston Dr. BT9	21	E12
Westrock Ct. BT12	14	D9
Westrock Cres. BT12	14	D9
Westrock Dr. BT12	14	D9
Westrock Gdns. BT12	14	D9
Westrock Grn. BT12	14	D9
Westrock Gro. BT12	14	D9
Westrock Gdns.		
Westrock Par. BT12	14	D9
Westrock Pk. BT12	14	D9
Westrock Gdns.		
Westrock Pl. BT12	14	D9
Westrock Sq. BT12	14	D9
Westrock Way BT12	14	D9
Westview Pas. BT12	14	D9
Glenalina Cres.		
Westway Cres. BT13	9	D6
Westway Dr. BT13	14	D7
Westway Gdns. BT13	9	D6
Westway Gro. BT13	9	D6
Westway Par. BT13	9	D6
Westway Pk. BT13	9	D6
Wheatfield Cres. BT14	9	D5
Wheatfield Dr. BT14	9	E5
Wheatfield Gdns. BT14	9	E5
Wheelers Ct. BT4	17	K8
Newtownards Rd.		
Whincroft Rd. BT5	24	N10
Whincroft Way BT5	24	N11
White St. BT5	16	J8
Whitecliff Cres. BT12	14	D9
Whitecliff Dr. BT12	14	D9
Whiterock Rd.		
Whitecliff Par. BT12	14	D9
Whitehall Gdns. BT7	23	J11
Whitehall Ms. BT7	23	J11
Whitehall Par. BT7	23	J11
Whiterock Clo. BT12	14	D9
Whiterock Rd.		
Whiterock Cres. BT12	14	D9
Whiterock Dr. BT12	14	D9
Whiterock Gdns. BT12	14	D9
Whiterock Par. BT12	14	D9
Whiterock Rd. BT12	14	C8
Whitewell Cres., New. BT36	5	H1
Whitewell Dr., New. BT36	5	H1
Whitewell Par., New. BT36	5	H1
Whitla St. BT15	11	J6
Wigton St. BT13	15	G7
Percy Pl.		
Wildflower Way BT12	21	F11
Wilgar Clo. BT4	18	M8
Dundela St.		
Wilgar St. BT4	18	M8
Willesden Pk. BT9	22	H12
William St. BT1	16	H7
William St. S. BT1	16	H8
Arthur Sq.		
Willowbank Cres. BT6	23	L12
Willowbank Dr. BT6	23	L12
Willowbank Gdns. BT15	10	G5
Willowbank Pk. BT6	23	K12
Willowfield Av. BT6	17	K9
Willowfield Par.		
Willowfield Cres. BT6	17	K9
Willowfield Dr. BT6	17	K9
Willowfield Gdns. BT6	17	K9
Willowfield Par. BT6	17	K9
Willowfield St. BT6	17	K9
Willowfield Wk. BT6	17	K9
Willowfield St.		
Willowholme Cres. BT6	23	K10
Willowholme Par.		
Willowholme Dr. BT6	23	K10
Willowholme Par. BT6	23	K10
Willowholme St. BT6	23	K10
Willows, The BT6	23	L12
Willowvale Av. BT11	20	B12
Willowvale Gdns. BT11	20	B12
Willowvale Ms. BT11	20	B12
Willowvale Gdns.		
Wills Entry BT13	15	F7
Shankill Rd.		
Wilshere Dr. BT4	18	O7
Wilson St. BT13	16	G8
Millfield		
Wilsons Ct. BT1	16	H8
Ann St.		
Wilton Sq. N. BT13	15	F8
Wilton St.		
Wilton St. BT13	15	F8
Windermere Gdns. BT15	4	G3
Windsor Av. BT9	22	G10
Windsor Av., Hol. BT18	7	Q2
Windsor Av. N. BT9	22	G11
Windsor Clo. BT9	22	G11
Windsor Ct. BT9	22	G11
Windsor Pk.		
Windsor Dr. BT9	22	F10
Windsor Ms. BT9	22	G11
Windsor Pk. BT9	22	F11
Windsor Rd. BT9	22	F11
Windsor St. BT12	16	H9
Winecellar Entry BT1	16	H8
Rosemary St.		
Winetavern St. BT1	16	H8
Wingrove Gdns. BT5	18	M9
Winston Gdns. BT5	18	N9
Witham St. BT4	17	L8
Woburn St. BT13	15	G7
Agnes St.		
Wolfend Dr. BT14	9	D4
Wolfend Way BT14	9	D4
Hazelbrook Dr.		
Wolff Clo. BT4	17	K8
Wolff Rd. BT3	11	L5
Wolfhill Av. BT14	8	C4
Wolfhill Av. S. BT14	8	C4
Wolfhill Dr. BT14	8	C4
Wolfhill Gdns. BT14	8	C4
Wolfhill Gro. BT14	8	C4
Wolfhill La. BT14	8	C4
Wolfhill Rd. BT13	8	B3
Wolfhill Rd. BT14	8	B3
Wolfhill Vw. BT14	8	C4
Mill Av.		
Wolseley St. BT7	22	H10
Wood End, Hol. BT18	7	P3
Woodbank La., Hol. BT18	7	R2
Woodbine Ct. BT11	20	A12
Woodbourne Cres. BT11	20	A12
Woodburn Dr. BT15	4	G3
Woodburn St. BT13	15	G7
Downing St.		
Woodcot Av. BT5	17	L9
Woodcroft Heights BT5	25	O11
Woodcroft Ri. BT5	25	O11
Woodford St. BT13	15	G7
Old Lo. Rd.		
Woodgrange, Hol. BT18	7	R2
Woodland Av. BT14	10	G5
Woodland Gra. BT11	20	C12
Woodlands, Hol. BT18	7	R2
Woodlee St. BT5	17	L9
Woodstock Link BT6	17	K8
Woodstock Pl. BT6	17	K9
Woodstock Rd. BT6	17	K9
Woodstock St. BT5	16	J8
Woodvale Av. BT13	15	E7
Woodvale Dr. BT13	9	E6
Woodvale Gdns. BT13	9	E6
Woodvale Par. BT13	9	E6
Woodvale Pas. BT13	15	E7
Woodvale Rd. BT13	9	E6
Woodvale St. BT13	15	E7
Woodview Dr. BT5	25	O11
Woodview Pl. BT5	25	O11
Woodview Ter. BT5	25	O11
Woodview Dr.		
Workman Av. BT13	15	E7
Workman Rd. BT3	11	L5
Wye St. BT4	17	L8
Dee St.		
Wynard Pk. BT5	25	O10
Wynchurch Av. BT6	23	K12
Wynchurch Clo. BT6	23	K12
Wynchurch Rd.		
Wynchurch Gdns. BT6	23	K12
Wynchurch Rd.		
Wynchurch Pk. BT6	23	K12
Wynchurch Rd. BT6	23	K12
Wynchurch Ter. BT6	23	K12
Wynchurch Wk. BT6	23	K12
Wyndham Dr. BT14	10	F5
Wyndham St. BT14	10	F5
Wynfield Ct. BT5	18	M8
Wynford St. BT5	17	M8
Moorgate St.		
Yarrow St. BT14	10	F6
Yew St. BT13	15	E7
York Cres. BT15	10	H4
York Dr. BT15	11	J4
York La. BT1	16	H7
York Par. BT15	10	H4
York Pk. BT15	10	H4
York Rd. BT15	10	H5
York St. BT15	16	H7
Youngs Row BT4	17	K8
Newtownards Rd.		
Yukon St. BT4	17	L8